RECLAMATION

RECLAMATION

THE EVOLUTION OF
A HOT MESS

LONA COOK

HOUNDSTOOTH
PRESS

RECLAMATION

The Evolution of a Hot Mess

ISBN   978-1-5445-2036-0   *Hardcover*
       978-1-5445-2035-3   *Paperback*
       978-1-5445-2034-6   *Ebook*

To my boys: Thank you for softening me and teaching me increasingly about life. I love you!

CONTENTS

FOREWORD

BY MICHELE PAQUETTE

I am new to the teachings of the power of the Universe and becoming aware of the energy that surrounds and composes us. My awakening didn't have an official start date or specific incident but all ties to one thing: my career and the end of it.

My job, my career, was my identity. Happy, smiling, creative, high-energy PR "Shelly." I was good at it. But if you stay in an industry long enough, you see the cycles. You see how you may or may not fit in with new models of business. You see others begin to position themselves. You must decide if you are going to play the game. The rules and people change, and there are heavy doses of gossip and drama. It gets harder and grittier as you move up the ladder.

Over time, my self-esteem sank, and my skin crawled. But I had a kid in college and a husband launching a business, and we needed health insurance. I persevered and played the game. I became miserable. I put out misery. I received more misery. I begged my husband to quit my job. I barked at my kids. I became a hot mess.

At the height of my work-driven misery, I learned my cousin had developed cancer. She needed drivers on her chemo days. I had hoarded a disturbing amount of paid time off (PTO)—because taking time off only led to being more behind at work—but I took a day to be with her. We talked for hours.

She told me how she was working through her diagnosis with the help of a visionary who was showing her how to refocus her thoughts for healing. She explained how this person guided her through life's challenges using the concepts of universal energy. She witnessed my misery and encouraged me to learn more and try talking to Lisa, "the Visionary."

My first meeting with Lisa produced anxiety, tears, relief, and a bit of disbelief, but mostly a curiosity and a need to learn more. Something was attracting me to it.

There were a few points I remember: be the light; see the signs; the Universe gives you what you put out. I pinned her down on advice about quitting my job. She told me bluntly that it wasn't a good idea to quit right then. In six months, something was going to change. Something would come my way. It'd be big and exciting.

Intrigued and desperate for relief, I went home and marked off six months on my calendar. I crossed off each month with a tick mark. I reviewed my notes every month, practiced meditation and gratitude, and worked to keep my misery at bay.

What happened six months later was indeed big: the COVID-19 pandemic. This was not an exciting change. It affected my work life significantly. This drove my misery to new heights, and now I had physical pain in my neck. #ThanksPandemic. Yoga, meditation, and walking didn't help. I was ready for professional help in relief of my physical pain.

Encouraged by my holistic health-educated daughter, I decided to try chiropractic care. It made sense, as I had met Dr. Lona a few months earlier at a seminar led by Lisa (the Visionary) where they discussed their cowritten book, *Awaken*. As I learned more about vibration and the laws of attraction and how this energy affects the physical body, I was intrigued by the idea of the connection of being in alignment, body-mind-spirit.

At the very least, my neck really hurt, and I wanted an adjustment to fix it.

As she worked on my neck, we talked. I felt tense, bloated, hunched over. Dr. Lona encouraged grounding, especially after working on electronic devices more than eight hours a day. That night, I laid down on the grass. I got in the zone (a strong beer helped) and literally felt little creeping bolts of energy sliding off my body into the ground. I became incredibly relaxed.

Needing more adjustments (and advice), I booked a package of adjustments, an investment I wasn't sure I could afford as people were starting to lose their jobs. #ThanksPandemic. Uncharacteristically, I didn't worry about it. I'm typically very focused on money and the fear of losing it.

But by this point, I was taking several days of PTO as required during the shutdown of some parts of our industry. Not how I wanted to burn my treasured PTO. The load wasn't lighter, but I was now in a pattern of chiropractic care, and I was feeling a little better.

On one of those days off, for no particular reason, I reorganized my husband's workshop to create my own space. I felt a small nudge to be more engaged in his business. I had been preoccupied and too mentally exhausted to do so before, but on that day I was motivated. It was fabulously fun.

Ironically (or Universally, if that is a word), the very next day I got the call. My job had been eliminated in an aggressive round of restructuring. The most traumatic event I had worried about had happened. I felt numb. I felt relief. One thing I noticed almost right away: the pain in my neck was significantly, dramatically less.

I cleaned out my office of twenty years, and with the car fully loaded, I decided to stop by the chiropractic clinic for a comforting adjustment with Dr. Lona. I knew I'd also get a dose of loving advice. She was not surprised that with the loss of my job came the loss of my neck pain.

I got a lesson in the alignment of body-mind-spirit. And then she offered me a position at her clinic. My fear of losing money wouldn't have time to manifest. Lisa the Visionary was accurate in her advice timeline. I started chiropractic care and met Dr. Lona in March, the month I was ticking off to. And because I didn't quit when I so desired, I left at a time when severance was offered. The disturbing amount of hoarded PTO provided a payout that assured me I could have the summer off and head gently into a different line of work.

The new environment would feed my need to be with people, embrace wellness (the core of my career when I graduated from college), and encourage learning more about the power of the Universe. Truly a new start. No more misery. This was big! This was exciting! Lisa the Visionary was right on!

It would be magical if I stopped here: how being in alignment and understanding the Universe laid the path for my perfect new life.

Not so fast, hot mess.

A couple of weeks later, I totaled my BMW. I spent some time in the fetal position worrying about the money to fix it. Then, I went headlong into obsessive worry about my husband's MRI because everything comes in threes for me. I started spinning out:

For sure, my husband will need surgery and not be able to work… my insurance will run out…how will we pay for it? OMG, how did I lose that job that was so miserable but paid so well?

Spinning with worry, I called Lisa for a quick session over the phone. At the very least, I could use some soothing words from someone other than my mother to calm down.

As I blathered on about my nonstop negative thinking, and my worry about putting it into the universe, bringing in more, and manifesting it, she stopped me midsentence with a series of fast-paced questions:

"Does the Universe have your back?"

"Well, yes, the insurance payout was significant, so I am completely covered financially."

"What were you doing when you crashed your car?"

"I was in a self-pity moment of why I lost my job."

"Was it a wake-up moment perhaps to redirect your negative thinking?"

"Well, yes, it was like a big slap in the face."

Her solution was quite simple. If you are not in tune, turn the channel.

Turn. The. Channel.

It's not as hard as you think to turn the channel from negative thinking to positive thinking, or at least neutral thinking. I started making a gratitude list. It's an easy way to refocus, even when you list things like hearing the birds sing (because you are no longer at your miserable job) or drinking coffee with your son (because his dream job was pushed back and he is living with you for the summer and messing up the house). Remove all of parentheses statements from your list. Get out the big pink eraser your kids had to have for school supplies, and erase those negatives you placed alongside the gratitude. It's gratitude, and it's powerful.

I can now say for sure I am awake, and it will continue to be a process. Learning, and learning more, because life goes sideways, and I have a lot of old stories in my head to decode. It's a daily practice. In the midst of a pandemic and riots in Minneapolis, my daughter, a member of the Air National Guard, was activated to assist with COVID-19 testing and potentially riot control.

She could not afford to pay for an apartment in St. Paul that she would not be living in. At the same time, my son's lease in Minneapolis was up. That last weekend in May, I chose strength over fear and packed up their apartments in one fell swoop. My husband needed surgery, and instead of focusing on the bills that would inevitably come, I turned the channel of my thinking, accepted what lay in front of me, and continued to manifest health, wellness, and incoming financial streams.

He healed quickly, and the checks came in without pause. As I was starting a new job for the first time in twenty years, I felt like I was navigating a foreign country. However, I was ready for the challenge. My husband and son decided to buy back my beloved car, use the insurance money to get parts, and fix it themselves. It was their way of showing their love for me, acknowledging my sadness and giving me huge joy.

I'm learning not to project misery. And as I don't project misery, there is no hot mess. Now, I can look in the mirror and see a smiling, creative, happy, high-energy Shelly, and she's awesome (I say that out loud a lot now). The only hot mess in front of me right now is the one in my kitchen at dinnertime. I can handle that.

PART 1

HOLD UP!

CHAPTER 1

A GUN TO THE RIBS

Thankfully, it happened so quickly, I didn't have time to think right then. (Now I have run through the experience many times in my head.) It happened in slow motion. The incident felt surreal. However, the whole thing happened in under sixty seconds. As fast as I didn't see it coming, it was over.

After they sped off, I stood there wondering what to do next. I was living in an apartment in La Heredia, Costa Rica, which I shared with a few classmates. *Should I walk back to my apartment? Do I just keep walking to the internet café to check my email?*

It was broad daylight—a sunny, warm, perfect day. I had been walking on the sidewalk (no more than a mile) to go check in on things back in the United States.

A motorcycle with two Costa Rican men pulled up about three feet in front of me on the sidewalk, cutting off my path. I hesitated, stopping in my tracks. They started to speak to me, asking where something was in Spanish. (If you're clearly a foreigner and someone picks *you* to ask for directions, be suspicious.)

As the motorcycle blocked the sidewalk, the back man jumped off and put a gun to my rib cage. I quickly took off my small backpack. Pockets emptied, small backpack and loose items gone. I handed over my things. I was stunned. (Luckily, I didn't have my passport on me.)

When he had jumped off, in that split second, I had felt something hard in my ribs and looked down. I remember looking down at my left side to see the metal. *A gun. Whoa*, I thought. I didn't even have time to register fear before it was over.

As quickly as it happened, it was done. Now I was left wondering what to do. *Do I continue on to where I was going or turn back?* Our apartment was equal distance to where I was headed. So I kept walking.

I sat down at the internet café and typed an email to my boyfriend. I also sent a message to my mom (but didn't tell her of the event because I knew it would freak her out). I hyped up my courage for my walk back home. I was a bit dazed, I must admit. I am not one who generally feels fear in any circumstance. In the past, I thought this was a good thing. Maybe it was not. Maybe a little healthy fear would be helpful. They did tell us not to go places by ourselves. Clearly, I had disregarded that advice.

Back at the apartment, I spoke with the woman who owned the house. She shook her head knowingly and told two stories of something similar. "Yes," she said. "If you see two young men on a motorcycle, it's a good time to go in the nearest store or get next to a group of people."

Little late for that advice, I thought.

Undeterred, the rest of the trip went on—we had several days of the month left in Costa Rica. I was down there for a monthlong rotation for grad school with a few of my classmates. Honestly, the last few days went smoothly, and I was happy to land back in the United States and be home. Feeling happy to return home was a new experience for me. I almost always wanted to stay abroad when I traveled.

* * *

So why does my story start here? Because this event stands out to me as the beginning of my wake-up call to live life differently. A gun in the ribs is a nice gentle nudge, don't you think? A nice "hold up."

In hindsight, the holdup was part of a bigger message that my life was off course and I was actively forcing my life in the wrong direction. At the time, I didn't know to look at this external event as a pause or opportunity to wake up. However, a change of direction was in store for me and beginning to unfold. What I didn't know was I could go along with the new direction willingly or kicking and screaming.

Little did I know, this was a major turning point where growing into my adulthood, learning to humble myself, and giving myself new chances would become my new normal. I was at the beginning of a steep learning curve, and it has only accelerated since as I have learned to witness the chaotic, devastating, and uncomfortable "miracles" life hands us as it says, "Go explore yourself. Go experience life. It's time to change."

* * *

This book is about bearing witness to your life and reclaiming what we all have at our core: a connection to this divine life that is ready to unfold. A life that is working *for* us, sometimes in the weirdest situations and ways. I know, if you are like me, life has to give you a crash course in order to wake up. I hope you enjoy these chapters on my life and can connect and resonate as I walk you through them. Most of all, I hope you can see that life (not just the highlight reel) has a way of cracking you open to your depth.

You are not a hot mess, but if you are like me, there have been many situations in which it feels easier to identify as a hot mess than a divine creator who is immersed in learning through life and its array of experiences. Most of us have not been given permission to view our life as important or purposeful. However, we all are both.

This book is meant to stimulate you to think. What is unfolding in your life, and why? You have an amazing amount of power and purpose if you can reclaim it. Let's start this process together.

CHAPTER 2

PAUSE

Would I have avoided the holdup experience if I could? I thought as I sat waiting for my airplane to leave the capital city of Costa Rica.

I think the answer was no. I had had a good month overall. The end of the trip had been more colorful than I had expected. That's all. It was just a bigger adventure than I had anticipated. That's what I chalked it up to. At least that was how I thought about my trip as I arrived back home in the states in 2009.

Most of my reflection on my experience in Costa Rica was pretty limited. *Okay, held up at gunpoint. Check it off the list.* It's not like I hadn't put myself in other interesting predicaments traveling before or when I had been drunk and out in various cities of the world. This had happened in broad daylight with no alcohol. Much worse, it could have happened to me many nights walking home from the bar alone at three in the morning in the United States. So, at the time, I didn't think much deeper about the situation or what the Universe was showing me.

Regardless, I was alive and headed back to the Midwest to wrap up grad school.

I was nearing the end of my time in traditional graduate school. Most of my classes were over, and I had three months left to do my final rotation and then graduate as a chiropractor. When I returned, I would move out of my apartment and step into the last rotation before graduation.

For this rotation, I had chosen to work under a doctor in sunny Southern California. (Sidenote: Midwesterners, do not go from Minnesota to Southern California in January if you want an unbiased decision on where to do your rotations! Too tempting!) Also, my on-and-off-again boyfriend was living there, so I had a connection and motivation to move.

So that was my plan: Cali for my rotation. Finish school. Then try to find a job. I wasn't too sure of my plans after that. The thought of living in the Midwest at that point had never crossed my mind. When people asked where I saw myself in the future, I didn't know. What I did know was that I was *not* going back home to Minnesota or Wisconsin after California. So less than three months from the end of my Costa Rica trip, I needed a plan.

In my mind, I needed to do something "bigger." I had a chip on my shoulders about staying close to home at this point. My parents didn't give me any suggestions because they knew I would make my own choice. Honestly, the last place on earth I thought I would live in my adult life at that moment, was my hometown of Chippewa Falls, Wisconsin. To be fair, I also think *no one* who knew me well thought I would move back either, as I had made it abundantly clear that I was headed elsewhere.

Enter the phase in the story where I eat humble pie, learn to stop being an asshole (keep reading), and begin to understand that life doesn't always follow my plans. Have you ever experienced that? The more you struggle to avoid something, the faster you pull it closer to you. That was about to happen to me. In the next season of life, my new favorite quote became, "You want to make God laugh? Tell him your plans." Even mentioning God is also sort of funny because I went to church during grad school approximately twice a year: Easter and Christmas. God (or Source or the Universe) or considering God in my decisions was not a high priority at the time.

I'll speed the details up for you.

In the next few weeks after I returned from Costa Rica, every single one of my plans for moving to California started to implode. My living situation changed several times, and I even lost over a thousand dollars on Craigslist while scrambling for living options; my Cali situation deteriorated daily.

Finally, on the last day before I was set to leave for the drive west, the chiropractor I was working for confronted me in her office. In her East Coast directness, she said to me, "Lona, wake up. When are you going to see you are not meant to go? If you need a sign, I am your sign. Do. Not. Go."

Insert a pause in my thinking.

My brain went, *What!? Not go?* (Also, this thought occurred in slow motion). *Whhhhattttt? Nooottt gooo?????* (Read in a deep, slow-motion voice.) A month ago, the gunpoint holdup had been a physical pause. A trusted mentor now was telling me to back out. I had not considered backing out before. In fact, I may have *never* considered backing out of anything. The holdup at gunpoint was a physical pause, but this was a new type of pause. A pause in my thought pattern. A mental pause. That didn't happen often for me.

Some of you are probably like me, to a fault. You're quick-tongued, quick-witted, can think on your feet, and are not at a loss for a plan. Ever. (And even if you are, no one ever has to know.)

In fact, for most people, you have too many plans, and they come *way* too quick. So the idea of not jumping into a next thought, a next move, or a next action is foreign to you. It's not bad to have quick thoughts and quick actions. In fact, many times, this trait leads to high success and leadership, and some of the world could use a little more pep in the step and willingness to jump right in. However, some of us (myself included) need a lesson in the *pause*. We need to learn to breathe, pause, and check in. And not just physically, but internally.

At twenty-five years old, the idea of backing down or pausing was a foreign notion.

Prior to these new experiences (i.e., a mentor confronting me to stop and having a gun to my ribs), not taking immediate action felt like failure. I knew one thing for sure: I did *not* want to fail. So rather than pausing or thinking critically about my life, I was always jumping into the next thing. This pattern of quick action was why my parents had also learned to not say much. I was like a bull in the china shop of life. I generally meant well, but I also could be an asshole if provoked or if someone didn't align with me.

For the most part, things worked out for me, even when I was actively making poor choices (more on that later). However, I didn't think about myself too critically at this point, or about what I was experiencing in my life and if I could possibly be making better choices. I also thought rushing into action was simply part of my personality; it could not be changed. Which meant I was not working on changing myself.

I thought my attitude worked well for me, and I didn't know how to operate in any other fashion anyway. If I didn't like something, I generally changed it immediately—*knee jerk*. If someone upset me, I generally let go of that relationship or distanced them quickly. If I said I was going to do something and it was my idea, it was as good as done. No backing down. No room for a different version of me to show up. High levels of protection and guardrails so that I kept steamrolling ahead. Sadly, I think a lot of overachievers get far with this mentality until it becomes their demise. They accelerate at certain things, apply this force to every aspect of their life, and avoid what doesn't work well this way.

I was great at coming up with a plan for myself and my friends around me. Which generally meant I attracted people who liked my ideas or at least usually went along with them. I could think on my feet and find solutions fast, which only added to my ability to argue or think ahead to "get my way." I generally didn't deviate from my plans unless it was my idea. Some may have called me bossy or said I had "leadership qualities," and those terms definitely applied to me in childhood and into my adulthood. These traits had helped me in sports and to usually get my way in general, so I didn't consider them a problem.

But as I was starting to realize, bulldozing and being the first to metaphorically punch is not always the answer. Maybe I didn't always have to know the next move immediately. Maybe it was possible that how I had operated in the past was not always what was best for me (or anyone else, for that matter). I was starting to consider and reflect on my decision-making process at this point.

As I reflected on why I was this way, I realized some of this mentality comes with being young. However, I think the earlier we all learn to see a new way of living, the sooner our world will change for the better. We become more dynamic humans. We also become less of an asshole. Or it might be the flip of this. As a child, you are shy and afraid to speak up. Some people need to do the opposite and learn to jump. Leap. Do something. Stop evaluating. Stop second-guessing. Stop perfecting. However, I was not that person.

After the experience in Costa Rica and the following month before I was supposed to move out to California, much of my behavior hadn't really changed. I was going to keep bulldozing ahead. On the very last day before my move, when my mentor really spoke directly to me, it shook me awake. I started to really reflect. What the hell was I supposed to do?

> Reflection: Pauses do not have to be long, drawn-out events. Internal reflection and using your intuition and inner guidance can start as a momentary thing. To many in the external world, they may not even perceive you have gone inward. However, these pauses can make all the difference in the flow and ease of your life.

CHAPTER 3

BACKING DOWN

As I said before, to my memory, this was the first time I really started to second-guess myself and my plans in a deep way. It left me scared. What was I going to do? Was I really going to move across the country to California or stay in the Midwest? Was I about to fall on my face? Was I going to stay and feel like a failure? I didn't know what to do.

Thoughts were swirling in my mind as I left my mentor's office that night. Could I make a new or different decision after I had committed to something else? Could I back down? I had never allowed myself to back down before (that I could recall). How would people see me? How would I see myself? Was I a failure if I didn't move out to California? Did that mean failure permanently?

In the moment, I was sure it did. And almost more importantly, where would I end up? So many questions. So much control I wanted over this situation, but I could not find it. I felt out of control with the fact that I was even starting to question "my plan."

I had many opportunities to feel out of control before then: poor choices with relationships, years of binge drinking, and lost memories pieced together the next day (or not pieced together). But as a youngster, all of that had seemed okay—partly because I was in that phase of life where others were living similarly. Plus, even with all the craziness, I was still jumping through "success" hoops. I was still passing classes and still anticipating what my "real" life would be like one day, after I had passed through this phase.

Even through binge-drinking and lost memories, I had never second-guessed anything.

It's ironic that what caused me to really get scared was this feeling that I didn't know what "to do" next. It's also ironic that this is where I really felt "out of control." All the poor choices I had made before didn't give me as much anxiety as sitting with myself and allowing myself permission to reflect.

(Sidenote: This felt so weird to not know what to do. For the first time, the next plan didn't come to me within seconds. I really didn't know what to do. If you find yourself in a similar scenario, pay attention. There is something massive for you. Wake up! This is the Universe giving you a pause. Take it. A pause. A pause! Let yourself go blank.)

* * *

So back to my story. I left my mentor's office in Minnesota that night and drove the two hours home (after crying, driving down the freeway) to Chippewa Falls, Wisconsin. My mom, bless her heart, was set to drive out to California with me in the morning. She saw me when I walked into the house at about nine o'clock at night. Seeing my face, she looked concerned and asked, "Are we going tomorrow?"

I told her, "I don't know." I walked upstairs to my childhood room on the left and laid on the queen-sized bed.

I was exhausted. The month had been exhausting. From the end of the Costa Rica trip to all the difficulties of trying to figure out living arrangements to everything I had to do to graduate. Not to mention swirling thoughts of doubt, ending twenty years of school, and now this: I was considering big changes in plans in less than twenty-four hours.

I felt blank and numb, so I chose to sleep. I allowed myself that. I didn't have an answer for what to do next, and I didn't care at that moment. I didn't talk to my mom or dad. I was not in a state to decide, I was too tired. At least I knew that. So I slept.

Then I woke up. For some reason, I knew I had to listen to what was hitting me in the face. I was humbled. I went downstairs. My parents were there looking at me with raised eyebrows. I am sure what I said next surprised them:

"I'm staying."

In the course of a month, I had gone from Costa Rica, getting packed up to move to Cali, and preparing to start my career to realizing I was, in the last hours, backing out on this dream. I was staying put in the Midwest with no future plan in place.

This may seem like a very minimal story. For me, this was dropping the mic. An impromptu change of plans. I had let go. I had backed down.

Previously, I would have forced myself to stick to my original plan and figure it out. I was good at forcing outcomes on myself and others. Surrendering was foreign. It. Felt. So. Weird. Relieving, but weird.

I felt tired. We now didn't have to jump in the vehicle and drive, so I didn't really know what to do. I still needed to figure out some things quickly so I could graduate in a few months. However, I felt relief. I took that as a good sign.

For the first time in my adult life, I didn't know what the hell to do. Also, for the record, everyone around me was not doing the same thing. We all were not moving on to the next grade. We all were not going to a college of some sort. We all were not partying. We all were not taking a test. What the heck was I going to do by myself?

I still had to figure out my last rotation and find a doctor who would accept me. I needed that done like a month ago. I still had three months of requirements to fill to get my graduate degree. I was supposed to start that Monday in San Diego to fulfill those requirements.

As much as I felt tired, I also knew it was not time to hide under the covers. Where was I going to work, live, and then fulfill graduation? I needed this all figured out in about seventy-two hours. I had made my decision to stay. The pause had been quick. It felt weird, but now it was time to line up the next moves. I had to start thinking on my feet again.

Reflection: Why do I tell you all of this? Because some of you, like me, need someone to put some rumble strips on the road for you and give you permission to wake up and pause. I am giving you permission to make a new choice. No one else needs to understand it. However, if your life is giving you the rumble strips, perhaps it's because there is a new choice staring you in the face that you haven't paused and considered. Some of you need to hear that just because you have always acted a certain way does not mean you are destined to have that personality forever. It is a choice.

A SIDENOTE FOR MOTHERS AND
DAUGHTERS FROM THIS STORY:
MOM: GIVE THEM SOME ROOM.
DAUGHTER: DON'T BE AN ASSHOLE.

If I remember correctly, my "nicer" self had decided *not* to tell my mom about the holdup. I remember thinking, *She'll only worry and stress.* So I thought I was doing her a favor by sparing her that particular episode right when it happened. I chose not to include it in the email when I was at the internet café in Costa Rica.

However, as frequently happened, my mom overly worried about everything even when I curated what I told her. My interpretation was that she was still trying to mother me, at least from my perspective. Two days before I was scheduled to fly home, I called her and was annoyed by our conversation. I blurted out what had happened on the phone. If she was going to worry, I thought I might as well tell her what had already happened there. Shock effect has always been a go-to ice-breaker for me in communication with my parents. It was an asshole move. Now that I am a mother, I can see that.

I came home a few days later, and not much was said. I'm sure she was worrying the whole time I was gone. I think that at that point, my parents had gone through enough wasted conversations with me that many times I know my dad didn't even bother to tell me his thoughts. If they wanted me to make different choices or see things their way, they had learned that speaking to me was probably not the best strategy.

As I returned to Minnesota and the end of grad school, life continued to get more interesting. The holdup at gunpoint was the beginning of a major turning point in my life.

Mom: Your adult daughters need some (possibly a lot of) autonomy. It is healthy. It's also healthy to realize the harder you try to shelter them, the more you invite their rebellion. This is a gray scale. There are daughters who would crave a mother's attention, approval, and guidance. I think many daughters crave that more than anything. However, worry, projected fears, and limitations are not the same as attention, approval, and guidance. We embrace our children growing up. Find pride in their capability, determination, and lessons that they need to learn for themselves.

Daughter: Realize you are no longer twelve, and you can choose things your mom doesn't always suggest, but you don't have to be an asshole by rubbing it in her face.

In my firsthand knowledge of myself, as well as a lot of other close humans (mostly women, but some men), it is easy to see how our society has created many adult children. Our bodies are adult bodies, but we are still looking to our parents to see if they approve or for our safety net and security. I was one of them. Ask me, when I have adult children, how I did being on the flip side. I am trying to plant this seed for myself now as a mother. Support and love are great, and so is the ability to leave the nest.

CHAPTER 4

CHANGING COURSE

I had seventy-two hours to line some things up since I had changed course. This is where odd things started to happen. By odd, I mean wonderful.

Of course, I still felt like a huge asshole having to call the doc in Cali and tell him I was not coming, but after that it felt different. The second I decided to stop fighting and pause for a moment (an evening, in my case), the Universe started to line up some different options for me. A new beginning unfolded.

The next morning, Saturday, I emailed a few clinics in St. Paul. One of the first responded quickly that they could take another intern. Perfect. I knew my girlfriend lived a few blocks from there, and she never stayed at her apartment. I emailed her to see if I could sublet for a few months from her. Yes, I could, and that would be helpful to her too. Perfect. I had an internship. I had a place to stay.

Even better, my new internship only wanted me to work three ten-hour days. So, I could be back home in Wisconsin figuring out what would come after I walked across the graduation stage.

All of this was lined up by Monday morning—less than seventy-two hours after I made the decision to not go.

Because I was starting to pay attention more to how events unfolded and how I felt internally, I was a bit amazed at how things had lined up so quickly in my favor after I had given myself permission to change. I still was concerned about what I would do next, but in the short term, things were starting to feel okay. Maybe I had made a good decision.

We are not generally taught that we can or should change ourselves sometimes; instead, we wear out our ruts. If you take one thing from this chapter, it's that nothing is set in stone. You can live differently. You can choose differently. You can embody a different way of being if you allow it. Maybe you are like me and take too much action with little reflection. That can change. It doesn't mean you are wrong. There are some amazing aspects of being the way you have always been. It's not a good or bad thing. There just may be other benefits from having the foresight that you can go about life differently at times. A change in course is permissible.

Reflection: Is it possible that you are too stubborn to see that you could make a new choice? A new action? A new viewpoint on yourself or your life? Even how you view your personality is up for revision if you allow it.

CHAPTER 5

MY EVOLUTION STARTED EARLIER

Before we move forward into my next decade, I need to go back almost a decade to 2002. You need some backstory.

It's important to understand that I had already been undergoing a transition, but much more slowly. What culminated with a gun to the ribs didn't quite start there.

Growing up in the nineties, my childhood was wonderful. I had so many wholesome memories, from summers in the pool with my mom and brother to family Christmases. My parents were great at being middle-of-the-road parents. They were not too strict, but I knew what was not acceptable. In high school I was a pretty good kid. I usually followed their rules. I was aware of getting good grades and getting into a good college, not drinking or doing drugs, not getting pregnant, etc. I was aware that partying would lead to not being able to play sports, and I was a good athlete, so that also was a deterrent.

For the most part I behaved pretty well. At least, in my mind I did. By the time I was leaving for college, I was ready for more freedom. I graduated high school in 2002 and remember being *so* excited to be moving out and going to college.

I moved down to Madison, Wisconsin, a.k.a. party town USA. I remember lying awake the first night my roommate and I moved in. I could hear the sirens and noise of downtown Madison (a much bigger city than my small hometown) and thought:

This. Is. Awesome.

I also remember that every chance we had, we would go out to parties. For the most part, freshman year was still pretty mellow. It was expectable. We partied, but so did everyone else. It really was fun. I had wonderful friends. We were having a blast together learning to live in our new city on our own.

I think when it started to get darker for me, it was a slippery slope. As the next few years went by, I started working to make money. The best way to make money in my mind was to bartend. I worked at one bar and sometimes two at the same time. I was bartending five or six nights a week. At one of the places, we were encouraged to drink while working. It was not uncommon for me to drink heavily six to seven nights a week.

I remember having a final the next day one semester. A light night of drinking while working was still seven shots. Seven shots now would likely put me in a coma since I don't drink much. That was a light night of bartending. I was pickling myself.

I was heavy into a social circle where drinking like this was the norm. Waking up and not knowing what had happened the night before was normal. Likely a weekly normal.

Bartender lifestyle in a college town was wild. It also created shame in me as I knew it was unacceptable in how I was brought up. My mom had looked at me like I was an alien or the devil when I was caught skinny dipping in high school. I knew what she would say now.

I am grateful I didn't go down the road of experimenting with drugs. However, I saw plenty of it. In this country, alcohol is pretty widely acceptable, and it doesn't have as much taboo around it as other choices. We do not talk to kids about how detrimental it really is to their energy and their decision-making. Especially in the Midwest.

I reflect back now and am impressed I was able to still finish classes and pass with decent grades. I worked a lot. I drank a lot. I tried to make up for lost sleep here and there. And I still cared about getting through my classes. By the time my senior year was wrapping up, I had become aware that I needed to get out of that toxic lifestyle.

Physically, mentally, emotionally, and spiritually, I was becoming bankrupt. I was carrying twenty-five extra pounds (from drinking too much and eating bar food). At the time, I didn't register that. I didn't know how unhealthy I had become.

Reflection: Have you had any periods in your life where you now know what your parents were warning you about? Have you had any events in your life that you needed to learn firsthand? I am sure we all have. Experience is a great teacher.

CHAPTER 6

NORMAL VERSUS COMMON

During undergrad, beginning my twenties, I was unconscious to much of what I was choosing. Wake-up calls during this period where I was bartending and in the bar scene every day were not hard to find. From waking up in my bed and not knowing how I got home and realizing I had actually been working (and now was wondering if I still had a job) to having new, crazy stories about myself or one of my roommates each weekend. To be fair, I also probably forgot more stories than I remembered.

We learn through experience. One thing reflection into this period of my life has offered is to look at what we consider "normal." When we have a false sense of normalcy, it is very easy to *not* think. This is part of the trouble with "groupthink." Instead of thinking for yourself or checking in with yourself internally, you do what the group is doing. I think much of mainstream life does a great job training you to just go with everyone else and do what everyone around you is doing. That doesn't make you less responsible, but it's easy to just accept the "normal." Then we don't have to think or question.

This conversation is to illustrate a point, not air every rough decision I made for everyone to read. But for the sake of transparency, I will recount one of my rougher memories.

My senior year at Madison, I didn't go home for Easter. I decided to work instead. Working meant bartending, which meant drinking heavily. That night was no different. However, in the morning, I found myself in a foreign house on Easter Sunday. I looked around. Didn't recognize anything. I didn't know where I was. On Easter. When I figured it out, let's just say I was not impressed with my choices.

As I sorted out where I was, I remember looking at myself in the mirror while I tried to put my night together and thinking, "Lona, you gotta get the hell out of the place." Meaning I needed to move. Leave the environment I had become so comfortable in. Leave the "job" where I was comfortable making money and drinking myself away.

Luckily, four months later, I did that. And in my defense, I had been thinking about staying and just bartending another year before starting grad school. This experience was one of the main reasons I knew I had worn out my time living this way. So I guess I did pay attention to some "signs." For the record, many "signs" are not going to be warm and fuzzy.

Almost all my friends also worked in the bar scene, so our lives and experiences were similar or at least relatable. Not all of them made as many rough decisions, and I am sure some were worse.

Partying, bartending, and heavy drinking most nights out of seven, not thinking about the sexual, emotional, and mental patterns I was creating. This was all very unconscious but, to me, "normal" behavior when I looked at my environment. Again, "normal" is not necessarily a gauge of healthy.

Something I learned once I was in graduate school was that many things are "common." We assume common is normal. It is not the same. It is common to binge drink in your early adulthood in the Midwest. It is not normal. It is not a health-filled choice at any age, and it is not without consequences to your life and what you are attracting. Our media and culture have much blame in making many choices seem normal. They are common but not normal.

It's rampant and very common to see sexual messages that exploit young kids. This is not normal. It is common to see heavy drinking at about every social function you can imagine—in the Midwest, in particular. This is common, not normal. It is common in Hollywood and in the media to equate "freedom" to fun and wild partying. This is common, not normal or health filled.

Reflection: What else is common in our world but not normal? Example: I would dare to say it is common to have disease in our world but that it is not normal. I would say it is common for people to have weakened physical bodies due to the lack of transparency of where true health comes from. But is it normal? What else have we accepted as "normal" just because it's common? Can you change this pattern of thought? Unlearning and reprogramming your belief systems is powerful.

CHAPTER 7

HINDSIGHT: A TRANSITION

As I moved into grad school at age twenty-two, I wasn't bartending. This was a huge improvement for me. I knew that late nights and alcohol was probably not going to be a good choice again. I was still working in bars and restaurants (as a promotional girl) but not drinking on the job and not working past midnight. And the money was still nice to have. This was a huge improvement.

I was still viewing life through the lens I had acquired from undergrad. I had a chip on my shoulder. I didn't trust myself. I didn't trust others. I was still tainted by human unconscious behavior that had occurred about one foot away from my face in the prior three years, almost every night, and my active role in it. I could not relate to some of my classmates. Some seemed too pure.

I felt like I had stepped out of a constant frat party and into "Pleasantville," a.k.a. chiropractic grad school. To be clear, this move to go to grad school and the choice to go into chiropractic medicine had always been what I wanted to do. Since eleventh grade, I had known I wanted to help people with my hands. I just wasn't prepared for the cultural change that going from a Big Ten university of 40,000 to a grad school of 1,200 would feel like. I felt exposed and different.

At Madison, I could be a number. No one in my classes really knew me. I could show up, take a test, and pass a class, and my social life seemed separate from my educational world. Pleasantville did not feel like that. It felt like I had gone back to a high school setting. I tried to just keep to myself.

Part of me, for the first time ever, felt exploited, uncertain, and unfit; I felt like, if most of my compadres in school knew what my life had been like the last couple of years, they would have rejected me. So I stayed pretty low-key at school. Went to class. Passed my classes, and didn't look to socialize much because in my head, I thought we were too different to relate. This was my own issue, but it felt real.

Eventually, I made friends with a couple of girls who I still felt very different from, but we bonded over studying and liking to go out and dance. I also had a high school friend I lived with. It was during this time that, as my life was becoming less toxic chemically, that other wake-up calls would start sounding.

I knew my lifestyle was improving overall when I started grad school. One sign that the transition was an improvement: I almost immediately lost ten to fifteen pounds. If that was not a sign that my body was glad, I am not sure what else was. I was not bartending and drinking every night. My system no longer carried that extra weight physically, and I was starting to detox emotionally.

.

Also, as I have learned increasingly about the mind-body relationship in these past years, I can see how my body detoxing and changing was symbolic for bigger changes for me as a whole. One of my favorite books, *You Can Heal Your Life,* was written by the late Louise Hay. It talks about how our physical body is very much an extension of our mental-emotional patterns. I am going to simplify, but "extra" weight is protection. The more you need to cover up or protect yourself, the more weight you carry. As my lifestyle cleaned up, so did my weight loss, and I started to heal.

I was unconscious to almost all of it. I had a long way to go to wake up to more of my own power. However, at this point I was aware that my new life in Minnesota was an improvement. Initially, I didn't love some parts of it at all; however, I did know it was healthier. I had made a transition.

Reflection: Transitions can be hard. They require change. They also wake up awareness in new ways. During a transition, what can you reflect on? What is falling away that needed to? What can you see from your new vantage point? Don't be scared to move into the next phase of your life. What signs have you been getting?

CHAPTER 8

HINDSIGHT: POWER HANDED OVER

Chiropractic school was an improvement for me. I moved to Minnesota and had healthier day-to-day habits. I was twenty-three. I had a very small circle of friends and, for the most part, kept my head down and plugged my way through classes.

I was in a relationship about halfway through grad school with a tall, very handsome, and very charismatic man. Everyone who met him socially liked him, noticed him, and was drawn in. I was also. Every time I would bring him to a function, people paid attention to him.

He was assertive and made it easy to just follow him. He carried himself in a way that made you feel like he had control. Many times, he did. He naturally drew people to him. When I first met him, even the way he asked me out was controlling. We were in a club dancing, and he asked for my number. I hesitated. I had just met him. While we were dancing, he grabbed my phone out of my hand, put his number into it, and called his phone. Ballsy. But okay, I liked it.

It was easy to be on cloud nine at first. The first months were a ton of fun. As I did more and more with him, a major red flag started to show.

First, several months into the relationship, we were out downtown partying. At the end of the evening, we came back to my house and went to sleep. Partway through the night, he woke up and went on a tirade.

I woke up confused. He was saying things about himself and me that seemed so weird. The comments were angry and about me, but also about who he really was. I had never heard him say anything like that before. He also looked like a different person: his eyes were narrowed, and his energy was all erratic. A Dr. Jekyll-Mr. Hyde transformation. I listened and at first tried to reason with him; eventually he passed back out.

I couldn't sleep—I was shook. Who was this person? Why did he say those things? Were they true? Luckily (or unluckily) this was not my first rodeo with alcohol and how people behave differently, so I chalked it up to that. In the morning I told him about everything. He didn't seem really surprised when I told him, which I thought was odd at the time. I kept it in the back of my mind but went back to cloud nine, for the most part.

As the months went on, this became a common experience. I could feel myself shrinking when it came to the weekend. Each month there were always at least one or two nights that some alcohol was involved, and those would be the nights I knew it was going to get interesting.

Like many people do, we think we can help the person or that things will change. I moved about twenty miles away from grad school to be closer to him. The closer and deeper I got in the relationship, the more things seemed not okay.

During the week, there was connection and support. On the weekends, things got pretty ugly. Not many people could or would see this part of me. I didn't talk about it. Some of my close friends had witnessed portions of it, but most of it was usually when no one else was around.

Most people didn't view me as a victim. I didn't view myself that way. I was strong, but I had a secret. My secret was how manipulated I had become by this person; I had given over my power. Mostly it happened through mental and emotional abuse on those nights with alcohol. He was way bigger than me, and one night when we were out, he grabbed me and shook me. That scared me, but not enough to do anything different. I truly don't even know how much he knows or remembers. And I guess it doesn't really matter.

Each time things would happen, the next day I would tell him what occurred after a night involving alcohol, and he would apologize. It was so confusing. It was like I had two relation-ships—one that was beautiful and fun and that I was excited about, and one with a very dark person who was harmful to me. I had left Madison and was drinking much less; however, I was still living in a dark cloud tainted by alcohol's effects on human behavior.

I remember one evening, I was driving. He had been at one of my chiropractic school galas. We were very dressed up and sup-posed to go out with friends after. He had already been drinking, and I could see a shift occurring. When this would happen, it was like the new personality took over when it came to me.

I think the alcohol allowed all his uncertainty, fears, and insecurities to come out, and they came out aggressive and insecure. Had I not come from a place in my own life with so much partying, blacking out, and unconscious behavior, I probably would not have understood or put up with this. However, I didn't fully judge him because I knew how alcohol messes with everyone.

Sadly, in our Midwest culture, it is so socially accepted that it's almost more taboo *not* to drink socially. I hope we see a change with this in our culture. I think it is already changing.

On that particular night, I remember driving down the highway with him screaming at me about anything and everything. I remember that at one point, he was saying how I made him jealous by looking at my ex-boyfriend at the gala and that I "needed to act right." And in that moment, it's like my personality split. I started to talk to myself in my head.

I wasn't scared (but probably should have been). I thought I was strong enough to handle this and help our relationship. I believed that this would stop eventually. However, that night, it was like my persona had split in two to help me see something different. I started to talk to myself in my head.

I vividly remember for the first time having a full conversation with myself. My empowered self was like, *Lona, stop the car, and tell him to get out now.*

My disempowered self was scared of what would happen to him and what I would do the next day. I thought I loved him. Maybe I did, but I think I was more infatuated, mixed with fear. Next, my empowered self said, *Did you ever think you would let someone talk to you this way? This is not you.* My disempowered self knew the answer to that but didn't know what to do.

So I kept driving. For the first time, I knew this behavior wasn't me. I also was starting to realize that this wasn't good. I just didn't know what to do in that moment. I hadn't really acknowledged that before.

I would love to say that I stopped the car, told him to get the hell out, and saw the lessons right then and there. Unfortunately, things had to get several levels worse before my brother and father saw the situation and helped me to prop up my backbone to make a change.

I had handed over my power. Before, my power had gone to alcohol; now it was to a person. I didn't feel strong. I didn't feel smart.

Lucky for me, I had family that, once they saw how toxic it had become, would not stand for me continuing to put myself in that situation.

The final straw of the relationship happened at my brother's place, predictably with alcohol involved. The difference was that time, my brother could read me and the situation and knew something was very wrong. He flipped out, confronted me, and wouldn't back down on helping me see the light. He also called my dad, and they basically had an intervention with me. It was not smooth, but it did happen fast.

I knew they loved me, and I knew I was not in a good or safe space anymore. When my boyfriend was sober, I knew he understood this as well. Things ended quickly after the weekend at my brother's. I knew why it needed to end but still had weeks ahead to figure out how to disengage myself on all levels—physically, mentally, emotionally, etc.

That period of life was hard on me. I cried a lot as I separated myself from the relationship. It was a really weird time. I felt lost as to who I was. For a while, I would look for him everywhere I went. I wasn't sure if I wanted to see him or was scared to. I had a visceral pit in my stomach frequently. I also realized I had changed my behavior outwardly. I used to be bold and someone who would touch someone's arm while chatting or give a hug easily. I had learned not to do that because it could have been a trigger for his episodes. It took some time for those aspects of me to come back. It took a while before it felt safe to be bubbly and outgoing again.

> Reflection: Have you ever handed yourself and your power over to someone else? Or taken power from someone else? Are you currently in these relationships? There is a marked feeling of codependence. Healthy relationships are not built on fear or mistrust. They also are not built on "fixing" another person, as that is futile. We get to change one person (in any relationship), and that is ourselves.

CHAPTER 9

FIRST A NUDGE, THEN A SLEDGEHAMMER

Now you see why a gun to the ribs was necessary. I needed a *big* wake-up call.

There had been other wake-up calls before. By the time the Universe is as direct as a gun to the ribs, chances are you have missed other wake-up calls. The funny and yet not funny part is that the Universe seems to have a sense of humor.

Subtly at first, the Universe says to you, "I am going to gently shake you. I'll be nice." Maybe it's subtle signs in your body. Aches or troubles that keep coming up. But you ignore them. Maybe it's small annoyances that keep getting in the way. But we brush them off. The Universe then says, "Oh, that didn't work? Okay, we are going to start to rattle you." Then it may be a bigger happening. A relationship that ends. Job loss. A medical scare. A fender bender. Let's say you ignore the deeper message still.

The Universe then says, "Oh, I see that didn't work. Okay, we are going to sledgehammer the crap out of you." These moments usually leave you reeling but hopefully ready to look at your life and self differently. And sadly, for some of us, that still doesn't work.

In my case, a gun to the ribs and repeated changes to "my" plans were enough, as along with some divinely guided people who helped me to see that maybe I wasn't where I was meant to be. Maybe there was a better way to live.

What I am getting at is that these moments were not subtle hints at this point. A holdup with a gun. A loss of multiple living situation plans in California. Money stolen through attempted renting online when I was scrambling to make a plan. Then, a direct "helper" who point-blank said, "You. Should. Not. Go." I would have been pretty foolish to not question things at that point.

There are always *massive clues* of what path to take, or how to navigate life, available for all of us. We must have the courage to look first, though. When your energy is not lined up with what's best for you, the path gets rocky—quickly.

When your energy is not lined up with your purpose and highest good, your point of attraction (or the energy you are putting out) generally gets interesting. You are a magnet. Discombobulated energy attracts the same in the outer world. This is the law of attraction, and most of us have heard about it and read many books on this.

When you feel internally imbalanced, your world gets more chaotic externally. This is a clue to go within. The cool part is that these interesting points of attraction are sent to you as experiences to help you get clear on what's best for you and reclaim it.

Our world has done a good job of helping us to "forget." Forget this power we all hold. Forget to look within. Forget we don't have to follow the same recipe. Forget our mind-body-spirit connection. This world makes it seem like the physical body and physical world is all that matters. Do not question your life too deeply. Just keep taking action. I lived like this for most of my first twenty-five years.

In hindsight to this wake-up call, I had not questioned much of my choice of actions or where I was headed in my life. I thought I was a typical college kid, and I was, for the most part. Especially in the circles I ran (some of whom are still great friends of mine), I *was* typical.

This is not a book saying that period of my life in my twenties was "wrong." It was not. It is a huge part of who I was, who I am today, and the lessons I have picked up. I learned a lot. I wouldn't change that. I just didn't register how destructive some of these choices could be for my psyche and sense of who I am. To be fair, though, these were lessons I needed, at the time, to figure out myself. I don't think I would have listened to anyone else.

The moral of the story is to start to heed your wake-up calls. I promise there will always be more. Chances are, if you are reading this book, you recognize what I am saying. You can see how some challenging experiences have brought you greater awareness and ability to change your life. You can see how these experiences were meant *for* you. There *is* no coincidence to what you experience in this human realm.

Reflection: What events in your life seemed to stop you in your tracks? Can you think of any? Did you learn something valuable at that time? What was it? How did you reflect on your own role in the experience?

Have you had any "jolts" or tough experiences that seem to be repeating? What do you think these events are offering you? I assure you, in every experience, there is meaning that is meant specifically for you.

The Universe is not just giving you nudges when you are out of alignment. The messages are not always about something that needs to change either. It could be showing you that you are on your path and purpose. How do you know the difference? Check your internal system. How do you feel? That is a great indicator.

IT SEEMED FUN (AT THE TIME)

The real problem I experienced with drinking, and I think many do, was that I didn't register the amount of trauma I was picking up or how jaded I had become. I had acquired a viewpoint on life and humanity that was through a lens of alcohol.

Did I trust many people? No. Given what I was witnessing and partaking in every day, I think most people in similar situations would make poor choices. Myself included. Most people don't remember their actions. Myself included. I was shutting down almost all of my natural power by the choice of alcohol and the haze it left my life in.

On some levels this part of my life had started out very harmless and was really fun. Like many things, there is not a black-and-white line but more of a gray area. But the fun was really about spending time with some of my best friends, my roommates, especially the first couple of years.

We could have bonded no matter what we chose to do, which, now in our thirties, I am happy to say we do when we get together. The point is, it was not all dark. But to be clear, as the years went by, for me it turned into such an unconscious phase of my life that that's what sticks out to me. When my college girlfriends and I get together now, usually about once or twice a year, we talk about how lucky we were that nothing more seriously dangerous happened at the time (that we are aware of). Yes, we had a blast, and yes, we are all lucky to be alive.

And yes, it has taken me years to unwind some of the unconscious behaviors that became limitations to living a better life.

CHAPTER 10

HINDSIGHT: HARD VERSUS RESILIENT

So now you know a lot more about me before my wake-up call at the end of grad school. Why did I go back to my college years and share those experiences? Because experience is the best learning curve, but learning from someone else's experiences is second best and can speed up the process.

In hindsight, I can see the evolution that was taking place through those years (and still occurring to present day). I was in transition from who I had been years before. I was shedding baggage that I had acquired. Still am. This is life, and this is what evolution is about.

I had exposed myself to a *lot* of lower vibrational states in myself and others around me. I had lost touch, to a great degree, to love, trust, connection, and states that are *life-giving*. I didn't trust most people. I didn't want them to get too close to me. I didn't trust myself. I still had much to learn to open myself back up to those abilities. Therefore, naturally I attracted a relationship that was not those things.

Some of you totally get this. You have already been there. You can see the difference of your life prior to when you learned to choose self-love and thoughts and choices that are in alignment with your higher self.

Some of you are still in these places, relationships, and modes of thinking where you are scared and defensive because you know you need to make a change, and it feels scary and hard. One thing that I can tell, looking at my life now versus then, was I felt hard. I didn't want to crack, so I got very protected.

I was hardened to myself and to my internal feelings. I was hardened to others. I didn't think too often about anyone's feelings or my own. When I didn't like what I was feeling, I made a fast change so I didn't have to feel it anymore. I was inflexible in that regard. I was not interested in deeper connection because first I would have to connect to myself more.

However, the harder we become, the more little fault lines are there to be exploited to help us break open. That is what was occurring. I was getting tested. I was learning new things. I was having to look at myself.

If this sounds like you, just sit with that for a little while. Why did you get so tough? It's not a bad thing, but maybe it's not necessary all the time. Is it possible it is even holding you back?

What do you want for your life? How would you honestly rate your self-worth and your own expectation for your life? Are you living up to that? Does the bar need to be set higher by *you*? Or do you need to make better or new choices to reach the bar?

The door to opening that is to recognize that life has many

options available for you in the future. Start exploring. Begin to dream. Stop placing limitations based on your past or current self-worth. Could you loosen up? Could you see your life from a different vantage point? Could things get easier?

For many, the trouble at this point is an overhaul may need to be made. For some, it can be small changes over time. Others need a dramatic change (like a move, a change in relationship, job changes, etc. in the external world and a major shift internally).

Last point here: no matter the change you make externally, you can run from many things. You must change internally. You must see yourself differently and have courage to seek a change. Then, the outer and inner world can shift. Otherwise, your internal attraction point will create a similar external experience again. Read this paragraph again.

In my case, after my troubling grad school relationship, I was humbled. I knew I wasn't as strong as I thought I was. I knew that I needed to choose myself and my own needs first. I again was reminded of the detriment that substances are to people's lives. I was continuing to get nudges to change and reclaim my power. It was about a year after that relationship that I found myself in Costa Rica with a gun to my rib cage and a change of plans when I returned to the United States. So now you know a little of my life before being held up at gunpoint. Let's move on to the rest of the story.

Reflection: Do you have a portion of your life that you feel hardened to? Or someone you are hardened toward? Maybe it's yourself. I have found, in my own self-discovery, that it always begins with decisions I have made about myself or against myself.

PART II

BACK TO THE STORY

CHAPTER 11

NEUTRALITY

The Universe loves neutrality. When we let go, that is a neutral state—less attachment to what the outcome is.

It's like saying I am not going to fight anymore. I am going to *be*. I am not going to push anymore; I am going to *be*. When we look for a positive during a challenging or "negative" experience, we are working to neutralize it. This allows us to move forward.

When I made the shift back to Wisconsin to begin chiropractic practice and the next phase of my life, I went back to some of my roots. I had to neutralize them at first. It was not my dream to move back home into my parents' house at age twenty-five. I was grateful, but it was a hard pill to swallow at first.

My frequency and magnetism had changed. Something in me had shifted at the core. Therefore, my life shifted externally. When I moved home and ate some humble pie, I started to watch what was unfolding for me and what was not. I had started to tune in to a different channel. I had taken the opportunity to let go and follow a new path. This new path was exactly where I didn't think I would end up. I was learning that this was okay.

I found myself back at my parents' house. No idea exactly what the next move would be after graduation. However, I knew enough to realize I'd better start making some plans. Throughout school, the idea of opening my own chiropractic center or business had seemed exciting to me. I liked the idea of running the show and thinking about growing a business and practice.

I started to entertain this idea more and more while keeping my options open. I also started to look around the area for space to rent if I was going to open my own chiropractic practice. I went to several cities and locations and drove around to get the lay of the land. I wanted a practice that would help other people in a fun and upbeat way—help them to focus on what's right with their bodies instead of what is wrong with them. I was open to creating this practice if things started to fall into place. I really didn't know anything about business but was willing to learn and get mentoring.

One of the spaces I checked into was twice as big as I wanted and painted like a dungeon (dark gray) at the time. For some reason, I kept going back to that space. I knew the landlord from growing up, and he wanted to work with us (also, this was right after the 2008 crash, so landlords were hungry for tenants). Long story short, I got a super-affordable fixed rent. They divided the space in half for me, and I had first right to the other half when we grew in the future.

What I didn't know was that I had unconsciously selected a business location that had a heavy traffic flow to it almost all day long due to the number of jobs surrounding it. We are located in an industrial and healthcare area of town and have the only fast food (Subway) restaurant as our neighbor on the right. I "got lucky." Or was I magnetizing this new way of life? Maybe it was a little of each.

The next occurrence seemed even crazier. I got home one night, after visiting bankers and looking at other items I was going to need to open, and a woman my family vaguely knew had called and left me a message on my parents' line.

She said something like this: "Hi. I am so-and-so, and I heard what Lona's trying to do, and I would love to help. I could answer her phone lines for free or help in some way. I have a free and flexible schedule."

My jaw dropped as I listened to the recording. *What!?* I thought. *Who does that?* It seemed crazy that someone was offering.

I ended up meeting with her. She was beyond "right" for the job—and highly overqualified, I might add. Her philosophy on life was so in line with what I needed to create; it was amazing. Again, I just had to shake my head and pinch myself. So she was my first assistant and did a beautiful job for years. She really helped grow me in many ways, in business and personally. I am forever grateful for her. She was truly a godsend.

Next, there was the bank. I had heard horror stories about trying to get a loan. I had prepared a business plan for two locations: one plan for the city of Chippewa Falls with the space I just mentioned and the demographics for that region and another business plan for the city of Hudson, Wisconsin.

Anyway, at this point I went around and dropped off my business plan at the banks, asking if I could speak with a small business banker about a loan. At one bank, I met a man who would radically change my life by offering me a chance. Jerry allowed me his time, read my plan, and then asked many questions.

At the end of the interview, I was sure I was *not* getting the loan. He had so many questions, and I was not sure my answers were satisfactory. Well, at the end, he said, "Congratulations. We usually don't loan for a business like this, but there are several reasons I will for you." He listed out the things he liked that I had said about my plan. And he also offered an additional possibility of a loan through the regional planning committee, which he would contact for me.

I. Was. Stoked.

I offer these examples because I am trying to show what a radical change my life went through in literally two to three months. Things went from a dead stop, feeling hard and uncertain, to a rapid flow of new opportunities rolling in. I went from a guy holding me up at gunpoint and all the doors closing to what I thought my future should be to *this*. I had thrown the towel in on my "move," and that had felt like failure at the time. At the time it had felt like I was giving up (letting go into uncertainty and more unknown). I had taken this change of plans and found a space of neutrality. I found ease and gratitude in living with my parents and being back in my hometown.

It was like every day there was some new, great surprise and new doors opening. Things that generally were "hard" seemed to magically to open up for me: a business space, a business loan, a volunteer employee? What!?

Reflection: Where could you back down? Where could you really let go? What is not serving you that you could just let go of an expectation before you know the next move? What signs have you gotten that it is time? Would you allow yourself to see that there may be a different plan in store?

DECISIONS

Trusting your decision-making is not something that everyone feels confident with. If you are really attached to a certain outcome, it can blind you to other options. As you trust that the right opportunities will come your way and that your inner voice will nudge you to make good decisions, it gets easier to navigate when life shows up differently than expected.

Not all decisions feel awesome. Sometimes growth and change will make you highly uncomfortable. It's up to you. Stay stuck or beat your head on the wall expecting life to be different without *you* changing first.

The point here is it's not all butterflies and rainbows. Decision-making is something you get better at with practice. Learning that you can decide and always renavigate makes it feel less scary. Learning how to line your energy up with your decision is also an art form. We all know people who say one thing and then do another.

Learn from their example of what not to do. Make a decision, and put your energy and action behind it. This will lead to momentum, and decision-making will become easier as you trust your inner guidance to navigate.

CHAPTER 12

SYNCHRONICITY

The years of 2009 and 2010 had so many lessons and so much growth for me. Giving up my expectation that I had to move away from the Midwest offered me the lesson in how to *let go*. Let go of expectation. Let go of the illusion that I could control everything. It was humbling. The change of plans left me questioning so much of what would come next for me. However, in the process, life started to show me magic.

We all have heard the word "synchronicity." Google offers the meaning of synchronicity as "the simultaneous occurrence of events which appear significantly related but have no discernible causal connection." But maybe there is a cause. The part I want to emphasize is they *appear* significantly related. In my estimation, the cause part would be *you*.

You may ask how that works. Why, when I "let go" of my expectation, did so much good flood into my life? Because my state changed. Some of you are still probably confused. What has taken me years to wrap my brain around I am going to attempt to write in the next couple of paragraphs.

You see, our life is not just a physical body. We are also not just a spirit and soul. We are all three: mind, body, spirit. We are energy that is physical and mental, emotional and spiritual. So we have dense physical aspects (our bodies), and we also have our life force or our energy that animates us. This is why a cadaver is different than a live person. The more I geek out on quantum physics and quantum theories and read more about this energy that is operating through us, the more sense life seems to make.

You see, each of us is like an individual tuning fork that picks up and is tuned in to a current of energy. Just like a radio station. We are receiving and projecting a broadcast or frequency. Quantum science is now showing us what religions, mystics, and more radical thinkers have been saying for eons: we are energy beings. We are more than our bodies. Our energy is what creates our world.

Our bodies act as conduits (tuning forks) for this channel of energy that we *are*. The "current" is electromagnetic, so it has a "pull" and a frequency. It is this pull and frequency that the Google definition is missing when it says synchronicity has "no discernable causation." Science is catching up and showing us that yes, this is a causation. It's you and the energy you are putting out. This creates an attraction—not only internally (your state, the health of your physical body, etc.) but also a pull in your outer world.

Ever have a day that just starts off wrong—stub your toe, spill your coffee, late to work, and bills are due or already late? It's like your frequency is set to something more negative that day. Once you realize this, the cool thing is you can become more and more aware to what you are "broadcasting" and change it.

It takes discipline. You must be responsible, catch where you are, and then tune it where you would like your internal state to be. This is synchronicity. Our whole life is synched to what frequency we project outward, our energy imprint in the world.

Reflection: Can you see the order or synchronicity in any of your past "accidents"? Can you recall your energy at the time or what you were focused on? What could be the lesson there?

SERENDIPITY

Life is full of things we chalk up to "coincidence." I don't believe in coincidence anymore. It's serendipity, and when you are ready to wake up, life will hand you more and more signs.

For example, it could be a coincidence that I was held up at gunpoint the exact same month I needed to "hold up" my life and make a new plan. It could be a coincidence that after making a new plan and giving myself a new path, life got magically "easier," and lots of weird happenings fell into place. It may be coincidence that while in the toxic relationship explained earlier, I started having massive welts on my back like I was allergic to something. I could not figure out what it was. They were sore and annoying and embarrassing. After I left the relationship, they healed almost immediately.

It might be a coincidence that during that same relationship, I kept having a dream that I was in my parking lot at my apartment, about to find the key and go inside the building, and someone would attack me from behind. The dreams stopped after the relationship was over.

You see, we can look at all these as silly unrelated events, or we can see everything as related. Your choice. I am hoping you pick the latter. Life will open up these situations (sometimes repeatedly, like a recurring dream) to help you see new opportunities, new ways of being, and a new destiny of life. The key here to remember that it *is* your choice.

When all of the above and more was happening for me in my early twenties, I didn't know how to look at life this way. Life, however, was starting to show me that I was part of this spiderweb, and the energy channel I was tuned in to was set to a lower vibration.

Serendipity or seeing the connectedness of your outer world to your inner world happens all the time. We generally only label "good" experiences as serendipitous, but they all really are.

CHAPTER 13

FLOW AND GRIT

Ease in your life is a beautiful feeling. Being comfortable in how you are living your life is part of this. To feel like you are on your path is one of the most reassuring senses I know I can experience. When my life took this new twist in the road at age twenty-five, I started to feel these things on a regular basis.

For me, it couldn't have happened at a better time. I was about to embark on my journey into entrepreneurship. To have my leg up on navigating my mind and my experiences with a bit more wisdom and internal reflection was about to serve me very well. You see, this "flow" and "ease" I was starting to experience came with actual practical value. It's energizing and helpful and will lead to expansion in your life.

Life becomes much more fluid. Action and planning are still part of the process. However, it's inspired action and planning, not just haphazard.

Let me point out the difference. Previously, I was taking action without paying attention internally. I was ungrounded. I was not willing to receive the feedback the Universe was giving me.

Closed door, closed door, closed door. I just kept going to the closed doors and trying to batter my way through. Hard work (and you feel you are getting nowhere). Ultimately, I always wanted to have a successful, fulfilling life and a successful healing practice helping people. Before that could happen, I was being offered some important lessons.

After my short pause, doors were opening. Things were flowing. I saw I had many choices. I didn't have to have all the answers right then (or now). I could abandon plan A and find another way. I didn't die from that. I didn't have to always do what "old" Lona would do. This is flexibility; there is strength in being flexible.

It also was hugely liberating. Many of you need to hear that. *You* are not your personality. *You* are much deeper than that. *You* get to choose. Want something different than your current circumstances? What are you willing to change? Who are you willing to become? It's not going to feel comfortable.

This next phase of my life story was filled with action, but the action was inspired. It felt different. It didn't feel as hard. There was still grit and getting things done, but it felt easier.

Find the balance between flow and grit. There is still action that needs to occur to create our most fulfilling life. Lots of action, but it can be inspired action, or at least action that is monitored internally. This helps you stay connected. Intuition strikes a balance with hard work.

There is a life-and-death cycle with all of our experiences. When we experience something that we allow to change us, there is a rebirth. With the rebirth, there is a death to the old way and the old personality. We can flow with it instead of resisting. We can teach our kids about this cycle of life as well. We do not have to fear change.

When I started to see I could live like this—where I allowed things to come to me instead of *pushing* so hard all the time— life really started to take on some magical qualities. Now it doesn't mean that I don't still *push*. Just ask my husband. However, I can see there is a better way. I can feel when I am pushing too much and I need to let go (most of the time). Let actions flow instead of always pushing.

Reflection: Are you gritting your way through something in your life? Where could you get quiet and look for a different option? Permission to pause the "push" can be very energizing.

CHAPTER 14

WHAT CAN GO RIGHT?

As this new way of living started to unfold for me, I simultaneously started to find more success, ease, and abundance in my life. In 2010, I opened my doors to a new business—a chiropractic practice. I genuinely wanted to help people with my hands and was so grateful for the opportunity when they scheduled and put trust in me. I also genuinely wanted to create this business through this new lens of potential that was unfolding.

Looking back, I had *no* idea the potential I held (and probably still don't). Do any of us? However, I was willing to get started and act forward. Inspired action.

I was no longer pushing by myself. I had some confirmation that I was meant to do this. I looked at the ease of securing the location, staff, and loan to open up and thought, *Yep, keep going, Lona.*

Of course there were setbacks, and there were weeks I thought, *What the heck am I doing?* And there were *long* hours. But it was my dream. I put one foot in front of the other, looked almost exclusively for solutions (not problems), and day by day started building this dream.

remember my dad, who was well meaning, told me, "Lona, this is going to be hard." And he would say that periodically. Finally, one day I looked at him and said, "Dad, that's your reality. I don't want it to be mine." Protecting your headspace is so important, and the ability to create momentum and know you are meant to keep creating.

So what if you have a dream (and I know you do) that you are building, but it doesn't feel like it's happening? Or doesn't feel like it can happen now? Turn inward. Ask yourself, *What am I scared of?* Your fear cannot outweigh your desire to create.

So many people keep themselves in the starting blocks because they cannot get over their fear of needing to know all the answers right away. It maims them. Another thing that maims people is needing approval. Don't let that stop you either.

One naïve thing I had going was I did not have a fear of making an action. Make a "wrong" action? So what? Renavigate. Other people don't think you can do it? Show them they are wrong. A level of mental toughness must be established if you are going to do anything in this world that is not deemed as the status quo. I guarantee there is no action you can take that everyone will approve of or applaud you for.

Most of the very successful people I have gotten to know have this in them at the core. They can forgive themselves for past mistakes and they can move on to look at new opportunities. If this hasn't been you, perhaps you can work on neutralizing some of the perceived mistakes and fear you have.

Play games with yourself. Instead of looking at what could go wrong, look at what could go right. This is a big headspace change for most of us. I could have stared at what would have happened if I couldn't pay back the business loan or if no one ended up liking what I had to offer. But again, that's putting the energy against yourself instead of putting your thoughts, words, and actions toward moving ahead into what you want.

So in the first year, I started making some money each month. We grew as a business. I could pay my overhead. I could pay my employee. I could pay my student loans. Daily, more people were coming in for our help.

It was awesome to see people's bodies change and heal with the work we were doing. This was part of my calling also: to see the beauty in the human body and its ability to change and adapt with a little bit of natural help. I also realized instead of being a doctor who told everyone what was "wrong" with them; we could be a practice that helped to work with everything that was "right" with the patient and increase health and well-being naturally. This was fun!

I hired some great consultants who helped me get more stabilized in this venture called "business" and learned more about creating stability and safety with profits. I learned about money as energy and a form of exchange and about how to move money better. Pay off debt. It was like a game.

I probably was on one of the steepest learning curves of my life at that time. Everything was brand new. I was twenty-five years old. No family of my own, no apartment even (living in my bedroom from childhood), and drinking from a fire hydrant in the school of entrepreneurship and adult life.

It was at this time that I made a good decision. I decided it would be best to turn new leaves in my personal life. Really limit my wild weekends and avoid them in my "backyard." In other words, be responsible, especially in the location in which my practice was growing up.

I was trying to keep the world I had come from further at bay. I still would go out of town and really let loose, but at least I recognized that this persona needed to take the back seat and eventually get off the bus.

You see, I still had a massive learning curve I would tackle later on—shedding deeper layers of this wilder identity and need for attention as the "life of the party." For now, the Universe was rewarding me for the steps I was taking toward moving my life forward and getting on with my purpose. It had become clear that I had made a good choice to come home.

I had wonderful support from my parents. However, being so young, some weekends I would duck out of our area and head to Minneapolis, Madison, or Chicago. You see, I was changing, but it was a gray scale of change.

These little escapes helped me see that I could adapt slowly to living back home and still be twenty-five. I would visit my brother or my college friends and then head back to my work-week as a professional. I also told myself I could always change and make new plans if I really wanted to.

So as I adventured into this new life and new business, I tried to keep my focus on what I wanted to create: what could go right instead of what could go wrong.

REFLECTION: WHAT COULD GO RIGHT?

Instead of asking a negative question about an experience (like, *Why did this happen to me?*), can you change the question into a positive? Like, *What's good that could come out of this?* Reframe!

CHAPTER 15

YOU REALLY CAN GO HOME

As the weeks at home progressed, the business grew, and I started to wear out my welcome in my parents' house. My dad and I started to butt heads. It was good timing for me to move out.

I had gone from living a life where I would check in with my parents every couple of weeks on the phone to seeing them every day with my life happening under their noses again. I am sure it was equally weird for them.

To their credit, their support helped me in so many ways those first months. I am forever grateful. From a place to land initially to my dad helping me in the practice with my buildout blueprints and my mom's support, it was all part of my success. They were an immense blessing to me and still are.

At this stage in the practice, my life was pretty one-sided. I ate, slept, and breathed growing the practice. It was pretty much the only thing on my mind. Ever. I had heart palpitations over the fear of missing phone calls that were coming in if the office wasn't open for an hour here or there.

My professional self was moving forward. My personal self was moving backward. I owned a business, had a professional title, and was making more money than ever before. Business was growing. Yet I was living at home, eating my parents' food, and asking the guy I was dating to come over to my parents' house. I was seventeen again. Grateful but weirded out, with more debt than ever and also more cash flow.

I think all of us go through this period at some point. This place where we have stepped into more of our "adult" self, but other parts of us have not. Some people are forced into this phase of life very early on in childhood. They have to grow up early. Others have not made this leap yet in their twenties, thirties, and even later, I surmise.

While in my midtwenties, I got to experience my family again in a new light. I hadn't lived this close to them in eight years. I hadn't lived under their roof for eight years. I had never thought of the different aspects of how I perceived life and where these habits came from, but I was about to get a crash course.

And so, after about six months, it was time to move out. I had learned it was okay to go home. I had to admit, even though we didn't always see eye to eye, it was nice to see my parents more. It was nice to be back in a healthier lifestyle again and an environment that was sustainable. It was also wonderful to be surrounded by people who wanted the best for me and loved me.

So when I moved out, I could enjoy being close without being in their house. It's funny how as you get older, you can relate to and understand your parents much more. You are able to see that they are humans with strengths and flaws too. Some which you have picked up along the way.

I was at a point where I could integrate more of my upbringing into my adult life.

Reflection: As we become adults, our relationships with our parents change. What has changed in how you view your family? Can you add more grace into your relationship? We all are just human with all our flaws. Grace for them. Grace for ourselves.

CHAPTER 16

THE GOD CD

About a year and a half into my life back in Chippewa Falls, after a weekend in Chicago with friends, I was remodeling my office. We were changing a layout issue; we had in the space. The contractor I had hired had been a student of my father's years before. My dad taught building houses at the tech college in the second half of his career. He had referred this contractor to help me. I also knew the contractor was quite religious. At times I was in the office doing paperwork while he worked away at tearing down some walls.

That evening, he came up to me and said, "I really don't know why I am giving this to you, but you were on my heart, and I think it's meant for you. I had bought it for my daughter."

I looked down. It was an audio CD (this was 2011) that was titled something about GOD and sex. Not exactly sure what to say, I just thanked him. I felt really weirded out and sat back down at my desk.

I was familiar with sex but not so much God. However, honestly, I was going to church sometimes since I had moved back home.

I was starting to be interested in understanding faith. However, it would be a far cry to say I was religious. So I set the CD aside.

Hmm. The old me (prior to the gun in my ribs and my awakening) would have tossed this and not thought twice of it. The new me was a bit dumbfounded. *Wow. The Universe (God) definitely does not think you are getting the message. So much so that your contractor has to deliver a message about sex. Listen to the CD, Lona.*

So I did. It made some sense. I'll sum it up for you. Disconnected sex (sex without emotional, mental, and spiritual connection) is giving a portion of your soul to another person and, if not held with some intention and reverence, creates a lot of difficult energetic ties. Well, yep, I could see that. That's the part of sex ed class they leave out. They prefer to just scare you with pregnancy and gonorrhea pictures.

I was learning so much more about energy in general at this time,. like how everything is energy, including us. So thinking of sex in this deeper way fit, too. I was also becoming interested in spirituality but was really struggling with some of it. Mainly the parts of religion that still to this day seem like man's rules to me, not God's.

So this "delivery" of this biblical CD on sex from my contractor had me quite weirded out. However, I was open to hearing a new message. I thought, *Okay, so maybe just press pause on my sex life for a while.* Maybe to stop dating altogether for a while wouldn't be a bad idea. That was the first time I had considered that.

Now I am not even going to pretend that my life view on sex,

connection, or yin-yang attraction changed drastically immediately. Or that I became religious. At this point, I would say I
increasingly become more spiritual each year but not religious.
Religion overall does not entice me.

The delivery of this CD and its message felt like another good
reason to pause.

In hindsight, looking at this pause in my relationship/romance/
dating self, I think it again was opening something up in me. I
felt like I was learning the art of discernment. Discernment of
my choices. Discernment of what's available to me. Learning to
look at multiple choices and not just have a knee-jerk reaction.
This again was humbling.

Maybe romance and connection were totally different than what
I thought they were. Maybe our Disney movies as kids set us
up ultimately for failure as well. So far life was not following
their movie lines.

I never took long enough to reflect previously on choices in my
personal life and my success or failure in relationships. I also
was not in a position where I was devoting a lot of my energy
to this part of my life. However, that would soon change.

Reflection: New thoughts, new ideas, new ways of behavior, and
even slight changes always open up a different trajectory. No
matter what, nothing will be what it was before. Life will be different because we are different. Change is the only constant we
have. Where have you approached your view on relationships
differently?

WHAT IS GOD?

When I enrolled in chiropractic school and started to collect some new mentors, I was also learning about the natural world and our inborn and Universal Intelligence. You may call this God.

I am not trying to be religious. Words are just words. The idea is what we are trying to convey using semantics. Words have different meanings to different people. I believe this power and Intelligence is in *all*. It's the quantum viewpoint or entanglement of energy and order that is literally in everything from a thought to a word to the timing of your birth and mine. Consider this: this Intelligence is what is "ordering" the actions in our bodies and our universe. We have a free will that influences it; however, we are not separate from it.

This Intelligence is miraculous. From the baby that is currently growing in my belly as I write to the pictures we see of the microscopic parts of us (cellular organizations) that are organized into these repeating, sacred geometric patterns with highly repeating numeric specificities. To me, this is miraculous and a signal of the Intelligence. I don't know how to grow a baby and organize all the DNA and growth that needs to occur, but my system does. This gives me faith in something bigger.

There is exquisite mathematics present in all of nature. To see all of this and *not* believe some bigger *energy* that is spiderwebbing us all together at this point seems too hard for me to believe.

I believe life is Intelligent and meaningful for our own evolution and the evolution of consciousness. We are all here in perfect order to add to this tapestry of humanity. Much of this book is about how to work with this energy of life. Take a moment to consider how your life is an aspect of this. Things become more magical. There can be more ease and grace in your life.

CHAPTER 17

A TAME BULL

Previously, as a bull in a china shop, discernment was not in my repertoire. It was now becoming my teacher. I could think before acting. The bull (me) no longer had to break every piece in the store. I could still be the bull, but I didn't have to be out of control. I was starting to recognize this change in me as I went into my second and third years of business.

I could be sweet and gentle if I chose. There were points in my earlier years where I didn't think this part of me existed anymore. I had become too hardened to let this part exist. (Now, I continue to work on this. My babies are helping me see this aspect of me.)

I think through the ups and downs of adolescence and young adulthood I had learned to display other characteristics for approval and protection. I also was brought up by a hard-ass dad. Not as hard as his dad, I'm told. However, we definitely heard the lines come out of his mouth: "I'll give you something to cry about." I love my dad, and even his one-liners are somewhat humorous. Still, gentleness and softness were not exactly celebrated.

Being tough, being a winner, was celebrated. The rules were simple: be quick, be tough, have the upper hand. Said differently, get your shit together and move on.

That's how I thought you were supposed to be in life.

This new way of living that was opening up since the end of grad school definitely felt different. It felt easier. I didn't have to force so much.

When I would go back to "old behavior," the Universe would sometimes show me a correction. I had a party weekend in Chicago and had been spending more time down there in the fall of 2011. What did the Universe throw my way? Mono. Slowed me right back down.

For me, these early experiences were critical to my development. The veil had been pulled back. I no longer had the luxury to be oblivious to my role in my own life. There was no room for victimhood if I was to be empowered. I got to be the master in my life.

As I said before, being more aligned with "the bull in the china shop" energy, to me, meant my nature wanted to move quickly. It wanted to go full speed no matter what. I was learning to temper that some. I was softening.

Around this time, I was also surrounded by a very masculine consultant group. Almost all of my mentors, consultants, and compadres were highly successful men. Most of us were quite versed in the mojo of "taking the bull by the horns." That way of life I knew how to do. Full speed ahead.

It was a very linear fashion of success. Here you are at point A, and here is where you say you want to go—point B. Now ge. there as fast as possible. A direct line, take-no-prisoners attitude. I learned much from this time period. It had its benefits; however, it was anything but gentle.

A new world of listening within was starting to unfold for me, and that new world didn't always go point A to point B in a direct line. This new world did not have "one way" to do anything. Eventually, I could see that I had to leave this crew as I was becoming different and listening to this inner voice more than my external consultant.

I was paying attention to my own intuition and was working on recognizing my own connection to the Universe. In chiropractic, we call this Innate Intelligence (what runs our unique life and body) and Universal Intelligence (what orchestrates the greater picture; the higher organization that is present in all).

We have all heard of the parts of what this philosophy of life teaches—things like karma, the butterfly effect, law of attraction, and intuition. But ultimately, I'll sum it up: all of your life is part of this ordered Intelligence. Every action and thought you make not only magnetizes your life and attracts experiences but also affects the rest of the universe because of the order/connection present in all. It's like an intricate tapestry, and we are all part of it and connected to all of it.

To this day, I am sure I still miss the majority of signs and synchronicities coming my way. However, I continue to try to see more and look for the hidden opportunities. It can be something small.

For instance, sometimes there is something I am forgetting. Like to mail a bill or to call someone about something for business. And some weird thing will nudge me to remember it before it's too late. I look at that as a sign. The Universe is watching out for me. I have the Universe on my team. So do you.

As I learned this way, I tamed my inner bull. I can go fast and hard. But I also can listen, soften, and watch, and that creates less friction and more ease. A taming.

Reflection: Are you more like a bull in a china shop? Or docile? Is there a mode that you "get in" that could be changed? At the core, we all have all characteristics. Some we play up more often. So do you need to soften up? Or harden up? For your goals and life fulfillment, you will need to be able to do both.

CHAPTER 18

MARRIAGE!?

I've caught you up on some of my life evolution, stepping into my professional career, and the first phase of my "new" way of living. So let's pick back up at the "God and casual sex" CD. After this small pause and review of relationships, I saw I could make different choices about how I went about dating.

I thought about connection and distancing myself from the physicality of relationships a bit more. Previously, that had always seemed to be the crux of the romantic relationship, but now I was starting to ask myself about deeper connection.

It was very shortly after this new awareness that I was coming home from a service trip to Haiti; a guy named Kyle, who I hadn't heard from in years, reached out to me on Facebook. He was someone I knew long ago, back in the early, first years of college—before I became jaded by bartending, when life still had some of that childhood innocence.

He had sent me a message on Facebook. I didn't see it until the morning. I called my best friend from college, Cassie.

She had grown up with him, and he was in her friend circle from when they were kids. When we were eighteen and nineteen, we would go back to her small hometown and party with her high school friends. He was always the one I had a crush on and would hang out and make out with while we partied or just had fun.

So I called her and said, "Guess who messaged me."

She knew, and she said, "Me too. He asked me about you and what you are up to."

I said, "Looking at his profile, it appears he has three kids."

She said, "Yep, with two different moms."

Silence on my end. *Ugh,* I thought. I was *not* interested in responding to his message now that I knew he had "three kids with two different moms." That was not appealing information, especially at my age of twenty-seven.

Cassie asked, "What did his message say?" I told her he just asked that if I was ever in Minneapolis, maybe we could ever grab a drink and catch up. She then said (as I remind my husband periodically, jokingly), "What could it hurt?" LOL.

Well, about twelve months later, we were married. Remember me stating I can be like a bull in a china shop? It was fast. In hindsight, it probably had to be, or I would have run away. Or he would have.

All initial chaos aside, my husband is a lovely, yin-yang balance for me. Truly a very mellow, easygoing character in most ways.

He also can be very stubborn on a few topics. Which means, of course, we butt heads frequently.

When our relationship began (and with that CD making me think slightly differently), I had paused and started to relax my thinking about what adult relationships had to require; it allowed me to go back into more innocence again. Poof! He manifested in my world. Someone from the days of our innocence.

Now, I am not saying when I was dreaming up Mr. Right, he came with kids, other women, and lots of child support. For the record, he didn't. That has been one of the hardest learning curves I will probably ever go through. Lord, help me.

However, his busy life with the kids and child support subconsciously, in my mind, took some pressure off me. I didn't know if I wanted kids at that point in my life (now, I am obsessed with our son and our new baby). I didn't really know what I wanted from a "partnership," and I sure as hell didn't really know how to create one.

I had already been burned by a controlling, domineering relationship, and Kyle was nothing like that. I had freedom. It felt safe. I think that's the value both of us could agree on. You do you. I do me. (This would later create different problems, but I think that's why it moved so fast.) He was kind. A good dad. Fun and safe and independent. I was all in.

I am not sure if you recall the time period in 2012 when there was lots of talk about the end of the ancient Mayan calendar. Would it be the end of times? We were not people who really thought about that much. However, we did want to travel and have a quick and easy wedding and vacation. We got married on 12/21/12 at the "end of the world." And on Mayan ruins in Belize, no less. Why? We saw it online.

I am laughing because, really, that's all there was to it. We were talking about a small destination wedding and looking at places. An ad for Belize came up. Both of us thought, *That sounds cool.*

Because we were one of those crazy couples traveling on the end of the Mayan calendar to Mayan ruins, we got to be in *The New York Times Magazine's* wedding section for the "end of the world" edition. Why did they let us in the magazine? Had I become Sarah Jessica Parker? *Pinch me*, I thought. It was a happy time. Lots of fun. Our mojo was running high, and we were attracting lots of fun things at a fast pace.

However, life was going to give us another crash course. We. Were. Married. That happened.

We did not even live in the same location. I had never lived with anyone other than girlfriends and by then had lived alone for three years. Now, we lived ninety minutes apart. Independence was key to the beginning of our relationship. So how did we become interdependent? It was definitely a slow process.

It's safe to say we are still working on that, years later. However, we are getting better at it. Marriage, in the beginning, offered us the tight confines to figure out that we sucked at interdependence and were going to need to put some effort into making this thing work.

I thought that by jumping into marriage, my habit of running away from commitment in relationships would be healed. I had jumped off the diving board into marriage, so that should say something, right? Safe to say now that I still had a lot of that to work through.

Reflection: Have you ever had a period of your life where good things were happening rapidly? How did it feel? What was your internal state like at that time? We can pay attention to these periods in life that flow and then learn from them. What was your energy and mindset like during this "feel good" time? Could you cultivate more of that again?

CHAPTER 19

INSTA-FAMILY

There was the issue of where we would live and how we would create a semblance of normalcy somehow, with our separate lives and separate businesses. I lived and worked in Wisconsin, and he was in Minnesota. We chose Hudson because it was on the border of both states. We commuted—a lot. We were never home. And now, I also had an insta-family every other weekend. Kyle's two daughters (with his first wife) had recently moved about two hours south of us with their mom, and his youngest daughter (from a separate relationship) had recently moved closer to us. It was a rigmarole. Meaning, a cluster. To his credit, they all were making it work.

In twelve months, I had gone from living single to moving and being married with three stepchildren. It was a lot. The girls were young and super-good kids. Adorable, really. However, from the get-go, most likely because of how things were between their moms and dad, it felt tense. Their moms were not welcoming, to say the least. To be fair, they weren't really anything. It was like I didn't exist, for the most part. So I stayed hands off. The girls and I had good times together, but Kyle and I had a lot of struggles to work through.

My first message from one of the mothers was welcoming (catch my sarcasm). Upon our engagement, she sent a nice congratulations on Facebook messenger: "You're ruining my daughter's life." Wow. Thank you.

I don't have a lot of advice for singles who marry into an insta-family other than everyone needs to be offered grace and space. You. Her. Him. The kids. It can be tough. In my case it was. You. Her. Her. Him. The kids. Tougher yet.

The toughest part was I felt like I had no one to talk to about what I was feeling. None of my friends were in this position. I was still in my twenties. Some of my friends were dating. Some were single. Some were married. *No one* had stepchildren yet. I couldn't talk to my husband easily about any of it, though I tried. Luckily, my mother-in-law offered an understanding ear, at times.

My own parents, I think, had a hard time understanding too. So for the most part, the fairytale in the beginning had ended quickly, and the routine of every other weekend being scheduled for us and long drives during the week to get to work had set in. We had extremely little time together for newlyweds.

In regard to my new "family," I learned it was best to basically blend into the background and lose my opinion. It did not feel like we were merging as a family, actually. It felt like he already had a family; sometimes I was a wingman, and during the week we basically worked.

Needless to say, the second half of our first year of marriage was *rocky*. We didn't spend the Christmas holiday together, and neither one of us knew what to expect. Would we stay together?

Were we already done? Had I failed? I didn't like failing. I think both of us thought it was the end. Neither of us wanted to fail, though; we just weren't good at marriage.

We had very limited time together and extremely different ways of communicating and arguing. We would argue. He would go silent and change rooms, and I wanted to have it out and get done with it. It would infuriate me that he could seem to go to sleep with issues between us that in my mind needed to be worked out right then. I would learn that it was futile to push.

I was in a pause. I was beat up. I didn't like my own behavior; however, I didn't know how to even process my own needs in this situation. I think both my husband and I felt totally frustrated, and we were figuring out that communication had to improve, or this would be the end. (It's safe to say, we are still learning to communicate eight years later but have made major strides.)

It was at that time, as I was contemplating my marriage and this steep learning curve that I was in, that my mom got sick. She was working in my office at the time (she had since retired from teaching).

I remember my mom coming into the office for an adjustment and telling me that she felt pressure when she would lie (on the chiro table) in her abdomen that she didn't use to feel. She went in to her MD for a checkup and was promptly sent to do all the things: consult, biopsy consult, surgery, and orders of what to do next.

I recognized some divine timing here. In the pause that my mom's cancer offered, I was spending more time with my parents trying to help my mom choose her treatment paths (she had the diagnosis of ovarian cancer). It was a distraction from my own life. It was probably not the time to jump out of my marriage. Kyle and I didn't have time to argue now.

So things in our marriage settled down. I stopped looking for a way to leave. I stopped staring at the parts of our relationship that were so difficult for me (or the focus at least dimmed while I focused on my mom). I stopped trying to force communication where it was not working.

In hindsight, my focus moved on to my parents and helping them navigate some of their decisions. My dissatisfaction in my personal life improved. It's like many of my mentors, who teach this way of life, who see things from the inside out, have taught me: what you focus on expands. Trouble is, when you are focusing on what you don't want, the negative expands too. There are great lessons there. However, sometimes the lesson is not what we think.

In the past, when I didn't like something or started to feel uncertain or uncomfortable, my go-to was to run (get away from the situation) or do something that made the relationship feel like it needed to end. For that reason, I was always the one exiting relationships. I also had never lived with anyone before and certainly had never been married.

Marriage is not so easy to exit. Thank goodness. I had to stay and figure myself out and then figure out how to be "in" a relationship—not always looking for a way out. You know the saying: you want to go fast, go alone. You want to go far, go together. I had only learned how to do life fast. I think Kyle was much the same. This was quite the learning curve for two independent people; however, life has a way of helping you cut through your own bullshit. My mom's illness offered that pause for me to sit and realize I was 100 percent part of the problem.

Kyle and I do have a great yin-yang match, which can be very helpful to see things from different perspectives. It also drives me crazy; I can see how balanced we are. There have been times I thought I would self-implode from my frustration in our relationship. I just wanted him to see my point, and I didn't know how to just "be" and not go crashing around trying to fix him or the relationship as the "source" of my unhappiness. (For the record, this is false. The source is within me—always.)

I am learning how to just give myself buffer room. Wisdom and more grace help everything.

It also has been helpful for me to think about my own parents in this. I can't recall them ever even arguing. I can think of one "fight," and that consisted of my dad saying, "You are driving me crazy." Then he slammed the door and left for one hour outside, somewhere. That's it. That's all I can remember.

So I didn't exactly have a good measuring stick for things like disagreements, yelling (more me than Kyle), being ignored (more him than me), learning how to be a stepmom (luckily my stepdaughters are great kids, and I am very grateful for that), or accepting all that came with my new household and working crazy hours with a commute. At the time, I felt extremely alone in this. I had to find some outlets to talk to. And eventually, I did.

What was happening for me was my crash course in acceptance and grace. I was learning to accept things that maybe seemed unfair or not what I dreamed of but somehow I had chosen.

Acceptance sort of felt like a punch in the face. I was not good at it. Little did I know how much more of a lesson in acceptance and placing your power where it actually can help you I was going to get.

Reflection: Could you cut yourself a break to not have to have it perfect right now? Where can more grace be poured in you for you or someone else?

TO FELLOW STEPPARENTS

In regard to my role with them, I felt more like a friendly, empowered female in their life than a mother. A woman who needed to be a good example, but not a "mother" in any form.

I imagine there are many other stepmothers out there who have also felt this way and many who don't. It would have been helpful for me to meet others and talk to them as I was floundering, but I am going to add this part in for you: give yourself grace. Forcing something generally doesn't feel good for any party. So I considered myself as more of an older friend and the companion of their dad.

For the record, most of us did not watch a Disney movie growing up where Prince Charming came with extra kids. No matter how wonderful the children are, you can have some deep feelings to resolve. It's okay. This is human.

Some feelings, for me, have been jealousy and unfairness of the clashing of how our lives have to "work" to make everything "work." Acceptance and grace for all parties in the situation is the best way I have found not to poison myself further, or anyone else, for that matter. Some days this is easier than others. All of us have feelings that matter.

Many times, especially in the beginning, I needed to breathe. I would step away for a while. It really was like the movie *Instant Family*. Trouble was, nobody really said, "Hey, Lona, this is hard for you. It's okay."

I certainly didn't say it to myself. I beat myself up. Still do at times, but much less often. Then, I projected my anger at my husband. I had this idea that things in a marriage were supposed to be "fair." I had lists running in my head of things that felt unfair. This was an idea I needed to give up because it was not effective for anyone, I might add.

Breathe. Pause. Choose for the moment what will feel better. Go for a walk. Take a bath. Go to sleep. That is what I wish I would have been better at in the beginning. Losing some of my preconceived expectations and learning acceptance was key. I wanted to fix the feelings I was feeling instantly. (Remember, bull in a china shop.) That was not going to happen.

However, the faster I could have learned this, the better. It doesn't mean that you have to stick with anything long term that is not working for you; however, accepting where you are currently generally lightens the load. So for me, acceptance was to let myself off the hook. I was overwhelmed many times, and just needed space. Sometimes I could give myself that and come back and feel pretty good. Other times, I just tried to take more space.

CHAPTER 20

WHO DOES THE HEALING?

This is an intense chapter for me. Outside of my evolution of marriage and three bonus kids, what I talk about next has been the most radically challenging and life-changing situation I have encountered. If my husband taught me the beginnings of being patient, interdependence, and acceptance, my mother taught me about unconditional love in a different way. She also showed me my lack of control—with the exception of myself—and how I respond and move into acceptance.

At the end of my first year of marriage, my mother went in to her MD because she had noticed when she lay on her tummy, she felt a lot of pressure in her stomach that she had not noticed before.

Quickly, she was scheduled for a biopsy of a mass. Ovarian cancer. This all happened the week or two after Christmas. My mother and father's world tipped upside down.

It was a wake-up call to do some things differently. A wake-up call that new decisions must be made. A new level of paying attention to oneself and different ways of living were most likely starting. A learning curve that would be mentally, physically, emotionally, and spiritually an evolution, if embraced. And it also would be these things for those who were connected (family and friends.) I think the whole world is in a great awakening to the bigger connections in our physical bodies. We are learning to look within and see how it influences not only our bodies but our worlds.

At the time, I knew way more about healthcare options (as my profession is dealing with health and well-being) and the various options for cancer treatment. Because my profession is holistic, I also had many thoughts about what my mom "should" choose and reject for treatment.

I wanted to scoop her up, immediately, take her to Mexico to start the holistic protocols, and do all the natural things we could to help her body. I also wanted her to start having additional therapies such as reiki and some other mind-body-spirit modalities to help her connect some of the dots internally that this diagnosis was offering her.

You see, when I trust this Intelligence, I don't abandon it when things are not going "smoothly" or flowing the way I would like. This is when I double down. The body is intelligent, and it's connected to *all* of who we are.

I knew her diagnosis had a blessing in it or something to show/teach her and us. We all were experiencing it. We were not having the same experience as my mom, who was physically experiencing it in her body, but it certainly impacted our family.

At first, I wanted to take charge. Swoop in and save my mom. I wanted her to do what I wanted. What I knew. I wanted to help her make all the "right" decisions.

One of my greatest mentors and friends, Lisa, who is a gifted energy worker, called me out. She said, "Lona, whose job is it to make these decisions? Who controls your mom's healing?"

I did not like what she was hinting at. I thought I knew best for my mom. Ultimately, I wanted control to protect her. I was scared of what would happen if she chose chemo and surgery. Being in the natural field, I didn't want her to make a "wrong" choice. I felt responsible.

What I forgot was that my mom is also a powerful being. She was and is capable of connecting back to herself and choosing what's best for her. Whatever *she* chose would be her path. I am not God. I don't get to know what this experience is meant to be. I get to be her daughter and support her.

To try to take control of her was not in anyone's best interest. Not my mom's or mine. I was learning (much closer to home) that healing is an inside-out job. We all get to heal ourselves. Someone giving up their choice to others is still a choice. Reread that.

So I sat on my hands, grudgingly at first, and waited for my mom to take time to look through her options. However, I knew my friend Lisa was right. We cannot heal anyone else, as much as we may want to.

Each of us is powerful in acknowledging that our point of power is within ourselves, and we can remember to honor others and our connection to them. I took my own power back when I remembered that I can just love and accept my mom no matter what she chooses. I can love and accept my mom even if she chooses the exact opposite of what I would like her to choose.

This lesson can be especially hard with our families and close loved ones. How many rifts are formed because we don't allow our loved ones the ability to decide for themselves? Just because someone does not "do things" or "act" the way we want or think they should does not make them or us wrong. As I accepted this, I gave my mom her power back (between us) by acknowledging that she was the healer. She had the power to choose for herself—and did a beautiful job, I might add.

We may think we are helping someone when we try to shelter, manipulate, and employ all sorts of strategies to get them to choose what we want them to do, but are we really?

This lesson was huge for me. I was learning how to let go, step further into my adulthood, acknowledge some of these attachments, and accept that I didn't have to be "right." I could just accept where things were. I was learning acceptance and to separate myself a bit more from my parents.

Reflection: Where have you given up control? How did you feel? Most of the time, when we relinquish our attachments to control (controlling a person, an outcome, or even ourselves), there is a wave of release. It doesn't feel good to control. Where can you let yourself off the hook?

CHAPTER 21

SOMETHING GOOD, EVEN FROM THIS

As the experience with my mom's cancer presented itself, I got to do a lot of reflection on my birth family. I had a lot of unconscious beliefs about how I needed to be in the world and in my relationship with my parents. I also had an attachment to the illusions of who I thought they were.

It was like I was still a child. I still looked for their approval. Still knew if someone had my back, it was them. Still held them on a pedestal. It was like, even though I didn't live with them and didn't need their support financially, I looked to them to be my emotional support and sense of security. I didn't need to fully "adult" because I still identified as a child. Their child.

Yes, to everyone else I was probably quite a successful person at that point. However, I still had not woken up to the fact that I could let my parents off the hook. They were just humans themselves, learning and growing, with successes, failures, and faults. So was I. None of us had to be perfect. I could let us all off the hook to some degree by waking up to this.

I see this also in a lot of twenty- and thirty-year-old women (and I am sure men, too). They unconsciously sabotage their adult lives because of so many layers of energy still attached to their parents. It goes back to that independence or codependence instead of interdependence.

I could feel that in my marriage. Part of the lack of interdependence with Kyle came from knowing (my belief) I had this "fallback" circle of "my" family, a.k.a. mommy and daddy. I didn't have to create a new family because I still was highly enmeshed in my childhood family role. That's not all a bad thing, but it can stunt growth in new relationships.

However, there is a conscious shift that occurs where your nuclear/closest family from your childhood most likely takes on a different role in your adult life. You are no longer "the child" (for the most part), and the relationships can morph in a healthy way. Prior to my mom's health crisis, I could not see how unconsciously tied to them I was. This foundation was only going to become disrupted further as the years rolled forward.

Our family relationships must breathe, grow, and change as we do. We are meant to be in a community and support one another. We are meant to have time to truly connect and accept each other. We are meant to mature and gain wisdom.

The relationships and love and respect in families and tight-knit communities are hugely important to our health. However, love and respect are not manipulation, passive-aggressive control, or pushing beliefs systems on others. Also, the only constant is change. Therefore, relationships are meant to change. Reread that if you need to.

It was like I really wanted her approval but never felt I would fully get it. And this need for her approval kept me bound to her in a weird way. At this point in my story, I was learning to really *see* my mother more. Maybe all of that was a false perception. Maybe she always did approve of me, and I couldn't feel it.

I still don't know for sure.

Regardless, the silver lining is that as soon as I realized I am my own person and my mom is her own person, our relationship started to improve. Before, we had both rubbed against each other at times. Recently, I had wanted to force her to make the decisions for her treatment that I thought she should make. But I changed and began to realize that she is capable of choosing what's best for her. She did just that. She chose a cancer treatment center that she felt comfortable with and then gradually added in more natural healing modalities than I could have expected. I was impressed.

As the months of her healing went on, I saw a side of my mom that makes me tear up even thinking of it. The cancer seemed to set her free. She spoke more. She seemed lighter, happier. It sometimes seemed so strange because I was used to different behavior from her. I think it was weird for my dad, too, at first.

She stopped working for me in the office, made a radical shift in her diet, and voraciously learned about mind, body, and spirit healing. I was so proud of her. It felt awesome to see her choose this. I was not pushing any of it on her.

Anyway, there was a marked change. For Jack's baby shower, about a year after her cancer treatment, I was helping her get ready, and I realized that my mom was happy to celebrate with me that day. That felt great. In the past, any holiday or family gathering usually came with stress. So sometimes it felt the opposite of how I imagined it should.

I could see my mom really loved me.

We all do this to each other, especially the people we love the most. Our own wounds or limitations hurt, and perpetuate those hurts, or keep us from seeing a different reality. As we heal and shift our energy, these limitations start to lose their power, and we can see them for what they are: untruths.

So I let go of control and started to see my mother as her own person—a person who has her own path in life (previously I don't think I had ever thought about her in this context as having humanness and faults). I got to see my mom open up and lighten up; she and I had more in common than it had ever felt like before.

It was weird, but by doing the opposite of what I thought— instead of forcing her, I learned to let go—I got what I wanted. I had changed, so my world changed.

We shared books and podcasts. She was meditating and connecting with her body. She lost weight; her diet became cleaner and more health-conscious than my own. Transformation.

Reflection: How have you processed your relationship with your parents? Do you feel you are in a good place of seeing their humanness and accepting them for it? We can let go of control of others and come back to our power. We only control ourselves.

MY OWN WORTH

We all have the power to change our state or our lens of how we see ourselves and the world. The feedback, or the channel I had been tuned in to, broadcasted and brought me wild experiences, risky fun, and a hardness that was a mirror for my own beliefs about myself.

Deep down, there was a question of my own worth, a question of my own ability to be loved that I had to come to terms with. In hindsight, I think I had veered off the path from who I was born to be in my mid-teens. I let outer circumstances and internal judgments overshadow parts of my light.

I still had a lot of "wins," such as graduating high in my class, getting into the college I wanted, etc. However, I also had some experiences that taught me negative messages about my sexuality and who I was. I think, when we look back, it usually isn't one event that we chalk up to "forgetting" our soul path or drowning out that inner voice. Our culture currently does a good job of moving us in that direction. Buy this. Wear this. Do this. Don't think; just follow all the screens that feed you what you need to know. Conform.

So we find ourselves at different points starting to ask, *Is this who I am? I don't think it's all I am, but I haven't thought deeply about it—maybe ever.*

Have you experienced this? Have there been some really rocky patches you have learned a lot from? How often do you listen? Have you quieted that knowing internal voice? How and when does it speak to you?

Do you realize that just like you have had experiences like this that cause you to lose your way, so has everyone else? Your parents included. We can cut our loved ones a break. No one has to be perfect. There is perfection in the mess of life.

CHAPTER 22

PIVOTING WITH MOMENTUM

While all of this was happening with my parents, business was moving fast. Momentum is helpful as long as it's momentum you want! Thinking on my business success, momentum has been very helpful. It also can be a little crazy. In 2013, I decided to start another practice. The first one was going strong; I had built that from the ground up (of course, with help). It seemed like I should be able to do that again. At the same time. LOL.

I also had moved an hour away from my first practice when we got married. In my head, I thought starting another practice closer to my new life with my husband was the next step for integrating our lives. We were in our first year of marriage. Both working a lot.

I thought I could just whip out another business, meanwhile keeping energy up in the first practice. You can see where I was headed. I had no clue the amount of energy it would take to do both. However, I had momentum going from the high of building the first practice, so I jumped in (remember, bull in a china shop).

I made the decision to open a second practice based on the fact that after we got married, I was now commuting one hour each way to my original practice. I thought I would start this second practice (five blocks away from our house) and then eventually be able to spend most of my time there.

I grossly underestimated how much energy it was going to require, and how much time. I somehow had amnesia about how much of my time, energy, and thinking power had gone into the first few years of the first practice.

I had a great intern who was helping me. However, as the only chiropractor, I really only had about ten to twelve hours each week to devote to the new practice, and I was still full time in my primary practice. So figure a ten-hour day there, plus two hours of drive time each day and two more hours in the new practice. Fourteen-hour days.

To start, I was open late nights in Hudson. I was working or on the road from six in the morning until nine at night, Monday through Thursday, and a normal day on Friday. It was unsustainable. Highly. (At least for me.)

Most people who know what I (with the help of those closest to me) have accomplished in a short period of time don't know much about this phase of it. I don't talk about it a lot, and they didn't see the early mornings or the late nights. The energy and action to lift something off the ground. It appears much easier and much more fluid than the days actually were. So why am I telling you this story?

First, because I still believe this was a great part of my path going through this phase. I opened the second practice. We started seeing people, and I was able to sustain that schedule for about a year and a half and quickly made some changes. It was not something I could have done much longer, but it exposed what hoops I needed to be willing to jump through next. My momentum was carrying me through.

It was a "mistake" to think I could do it without a lot of help. So five months in, I hired an associate to help me in the main practice. Then, about a year in, I found a great partner who would take over the second practice. I didn't have that in the plan at first. However, things have a way of working out if the energy is with you and congruent with a higher vision.

I was in a massive learning curve. I was learning leadership, adding more people to the practice and mission. I was learning how to make business decisions that weren't just based on me. I was also learning how to take momentum and pivot. Pivoting can be very helpful in business. How to decide and make it the right decision, even if you have to be on plan A through Z to keep things rolling. Learning to pivot and go with the flow is imperative in life.

How many times do we abandon something because plan A and B didn't work? Plan A and B just maybe didn't have the right mojo, life experiences, or bandwidth to get the job fully done; however, they were not worthless. They will be worthless, though, if you let the momentum drop. You must fail forward. Learn and keep moving. If you are listening within and making lemonade out of your lemons, then you will pivot. Pivot, but keep going. Know that a pivot may be a very slight turn or a radical shift. Sometimes brilliance will come after those rough days when it feels like everything is "wrong" or "too hard."

Reflection: What type of momentum do you have rolling? Do you feel your momentum is moving quickly in the direction you love? Or is it sluggish? How is that a reflection of your energy and action recently? Where could you pivot?

CHAPTER 23

NEW LIFE, NEW LOVE.

I settled into my marriage; we survived the learning curve in the first couple of years. There were some very good times, and there were quite a few hard times. However, I could see I was changing. I was working on changing. Things started to feel better. Love and figuring out love were changing me.

It was also around this time I decided that I *did* want to have a child of my own. As much as my stepdaughters are beautiful kids, I did not birth them, and we really had separate lives. Kyle and I had our life when they were with us and our kidless life most of the time.

As this was all happening, I was starting to have desires about having my own child. This was really the first time I had thought deeply about having children in my life. I think my husband already having kids gave me a free pass to choose either way and not feel pressure. But now I was starting to feel certain that I *did* want to.

We got pregnant almost immediately, and I was convinced (more than hopeful, too) that it was a boy. I didn't exactly know how to connect with the little being inside of me, but I did know I wanted him.

My willingness to stay, look at myself, and work on my relationship had led me to a point where I felt comfortable being responsible for bringing another human into the picture. I was excited to see who would choose us.

I went into beginning labor in the early morning hours, and Jack was born about twenty-two hours later at home with Karen, the midwife. It was and is the best experience of my life to date.

Whoa! You hear all the clichés about how kids change you. It's true! I think almost every big occurrence in your life changes you. Birthing my business changed me. Birthing myself into a wife changed me. Birthing myself back into my adult life "back home" changed me. And this was no different. Becoming Jack's mama changed me.

* * *

I was in the fast lane of learning about love and trust. First, it was the experience of birthing a child. The slow progress of growing a baby in your belly, then the contractions, the intensity of labor, and, in Jack's case, being fully aware of him coming out (with some help from my ninja midwife who, in the last moments, picked me up and flipped me over when I told her I was too tired to do it myself).

I saw him as she set him on a blanket on the blue bathroom floor in front of me. A boy! Jack! He was staring at me with a furrowed brow. Not crying. Eyes wide open. Looking at me, a little like, *Mom, what the hell took so long?* I tell him this now.

He laughs. He still furrows his brow frequently and is an inte little teacher. He speaks his mind. Little did I know, when you give birth, you birth your greatest teachers.

Little did I know, also, what this deep love would feel like. One of my best friends said to me, "When you birth, it's like your love is walking around outside of your body." She was right. It's beautiful. And wild. Talk about the Intelligence and order in this world. It's radical!

To feel love at this level is a gift. It spreads. Once you know deeper love, you can apply it to so many other areas of your life and your perceptions. My love for Jack helped me to soften. Helped me to feel more of all the other emotions out there. Helped me to see what unconditional love could really feel like and to trust the process that was unfolding me and bringing me to these new places in my life.

Reflection: What in your life has radically changed from having kids? Maybe you don't have physical babies, but is there anything you feel you have birthed? An idea? A business? Yourself? How has this birthing been an act of love? How has it changed you?

CHAPTER 24

MENTORS

Birthing. In my case, it was also like a Mack truck hit me. Holy hell was I sore for days! And then, your boobs! Nobody tells new moms about what their body is going to do. You think transformation of your body happens *during* the pregnancy? You've got another thing coming after you deliver the baby!

The milk coming in, your uterus shrinking. Your body almost exclusively belongs to this new being day and night. It's both truly amazing and overwhelming. This is also why having an older woman or women who have been there before to support you, tell you, show you, and calm you is *so important.*

There are so many aspects in life that having a sister, mother, grandma, mentor, friend, another woman, or human who can mentor you is priceless. This is part of my writing this book. If another person can learn from me or I can lessen the load you have to carry, this is why I am writing. Many have lessened my load. We all have things we can share with others.

I totally support women finding their voices to help other women. Yes, 100 percent, I am all for that. I am for *all* humans helping other humans. However, especially to teach other women to birth, nurse, and step into our "new" roles. To help us do what is already natural to us as part of Mother Nature. We just might need a reminder and some help. This is so important for our culture and future generations. The planet needs all of us to share in our collective empowerment. We are one.

Thank *God* for my midwife. I borrowed her certainty for the birth, nursing, and motherhood. She baptized me into faith in myself—that I could do this thing called birth. That is more innate to our being than almost anything. That my core already had the power to birth, nurse, and do the things I would need to do for a child.

I wore her certainty for a while. Now I can do that for others. So can you. There is something you have to offer that would help elevate humanity by you being present in this tapestry of humans right now. Are you sharing it? Life is going to try to pull it out of you one way or another.

During the second pregnancy, my midwife's confidence had become my own. I know my new baby is a teacher for me as well. Fear still can creep up into my experience, but I register that it, too, is a mentor for me. Fear is not all bad. It is part of our survival instinct. However, feeling fear, leaning into my mentor's teachings, and feeling my own strength is a muscle I choose to keep flexing.

Reflection: Think back. Who have been your biggest mentors? Who helped you to set yourself free to be more authentically you? Have you honored them? Pay a tribute to those who have made an impact in your life. It could be as simple as sending them an intention of gratitude.

CHAPTER 25

PUTTING THE PARTY
GIRL TO BED

When Jack was born, a part of me that I had still been struggling with (and was hanging on by a thread) was ready to die. Finally, the party girl was no longer a part of me; she had no desire to stay alive. The pregnancy, shy of nine months, was the first time since I had left for undergrad that I had gone a week without alcohol of any sort in my system. My system had gotten nine months to clean out from the *very* socially approved depressant.

Now I am not trying to make alcohol seem utterly terrible. When I am not pregnant, I still like to have a glass of wine here and there (some weeks more than others). However, I would guess for almost everyone, if they are really being honest, there is not a lot of good or forward momentum that alcohol brings into their lives. For myself, I knew that to be true by that point in my life. So when Jack came into this world, the desire to be "drunk" had lost its appeal.

Some people, myself included, prior to this epiphany, would have argued that I had no "issues" with it. Drinking is just fun.

Right. Until it's not fun. There is usually a point where the fun (or your mouth or your actions) becomes a bit (or a lot) out of control. And whether that's happening weekly or every twelve months, it really can impact your life negatively. Problem is, it's tough to see it while you are in it.

Since Jack's entrance into the world, I have a much, much, much healthier relationship with alcohol. I have "socially distanced" myself from it. I can be in proximity without feeling like I need to be drunk. I don't think I really could do that before. I can have one drink and be done. I can go a month and have no alcohol. It feels good to transform this part of my life.

During pregnancy, it gave me time to really reflect on my relationship with drinking. I wouldn't have done those nine months for myself, but I would for my child. Sometimes our love for others trumps our love for ourselves in a way that can motivate us to make better choices.

Watching my husband's evolution with alcohol has been similar, although with different timing. As alcohol becomes less a part of his life, our marriage is better. The choices we make are much better for the longevity of this family. And honestly, I think we can see there were some glaring issues that our alcohol usage brought out in us.

So why have I spent so much time on this one topic? First, because I think many people can relate (whether they want to or not).

Second, if you are (like I was/am) on a path where your life is accelerating in a good way, you become more awake to your choices. As you do this, you are more successful, and you are choosing your actions based on what is *best* for you and those helping you to create your life.

As I distanced myself from drunken adventures, I was much calmer in my life. My financial life, love life, health, satisfaction, and purpose have all increased. I chalk this up to my energy being more *for* what I want in my life, so I am attracting better life scenarios and can recognize more of my true self.

Last point: of course my parents had tried to tell me this all along. Most of us learn through trial and error. It's great if we can pick up hints before we have to live them. However, whether it's your parents, reading this book, or other conversations that open up a new idea in your mind, this is how you decide at some point to make a change. The change then comes from you.

We all "know" better in many life decisions, even when we choose not to act better. Eating better food, exercising, letting go of stress—the choices are up to you.

Remember we talked about how life is happening through us and we are like magnets for our circumstances? (This is not foo-foo. It's science: quantum biology. Some of my favorite people to read on this subject are Dr. Bruce Lipton, Dr. Joe Dispenza, Dr. Lynne McTaggart, and Dr. David Hawkins. Can you tell I geek out?) When you're drunk or on depressants or any majorly altering chemical, it majorly messes with your frequency and what you're attracting.

As you make some of these transformations, people may change with you. Some will not. If they are not changing, try to make some new friends. You know what they say: birds of a feather flock together. Pay attention to that as well. It doesn't have to be cutthroat, but there can be a handful of friends and family you choose to be around less. It is sometimes not in your best interest to try to save relationships with everyone you have previously been connected to. Keep that in mind.

So by this point, I was ready to put the party girl to bed. For good.

Reflection: Is there an aspect of your persona you have put to bed? Or maybe you need to wake up? Is there something you are avoiding changing but know for your life to improve, it must change? Remember we get to choose and change. What once was does not always have to be.

CHAPTER 26

RADICAL LOVE

With my son, I dropped my attachment to partying. More importantly, there was this *love*! Oh my, this love.

I love that little boy like nothing else I have experienced. I am sure it's nauseating to others at times. However, to have anything, a person, an idea, or something in this world that you can unconditionally love is a beautiful experience. It's so pure. It softens you. It makes you vulnerable. It opens you up. It's wonderful and scary.

That is probably the next biggest aspect of me that changed. I opened up. I softened. I was no longer a lean solo machine.

I had a child I wanted and loved. Yes, I was married before Jack came along, but we functioned pretty independently. Now my life was transformed by this tiny human. I was also vulnerable because of this love. And for the first time, I was okay with vulnerability. Before, vulnerability had meant unsafe. Now it had a reward. This love.

There is so much power in sharing your vulnerabilities. And

there can still be a balance. You can have strength, power, even a warrior quality and still show your authenticity and vulnerabilities at appropriate times. This makes you much more fully human and helps others.

You see, we all have these qualities. It's just that most of us have gotten really good at hiding them. What's pure gold is if you have cultivated one or two or a group of people you feel safe with. That will allow you to be many flavors of human. We can offer that to those we love—really see and accept them for their different facets and hold them accountable to their potential.

You do this with your child. They are snuggly…you love them. They are crying…you love them. They talk back…you love them. They poop on you…you love them. They say something mean… you love them. You get my point.

The experience of this unconditional love is so wonderful. Some people are easy to love. Others are not. Some people give and receive love easily. Others do not. Wherever you register on that continuum, you are worthy of love.

Children crack us open to love. However, ultimately feeling love for even our deepest challenges or our perceived "haters" is part of moving into unconditional love. We set ourselves free when we send more love out in the world.

If these thoughts make you uncomfortable (i.e., sending and receiving more love, loving your "enemy"), then it's probably okay to just take baby steps. Maybe instead of "love," you "tolerate." That could be a step in the right direction.

Reflection: Can you think of your own experiences with love? Have you shut off further (like I had in the past), or have you opened up from these experiences? Has sharing love ever made you uncomfortable? I like to acknowledge (i.e., via affirmation) frequently that I deserve to be loved. That I am loving and lovable.

CHAPTER 27

MILK. MO' MILK

So another topic with birth. Breastfeeding. As not a well-endowed female, it was like, *Whoa! What has happened to my chest?* Throughout pregnancy, it was kind of amazing to see. Then, a day after Jack's birth, when my milk came in, holy bananas.

It was alarming. My chest seemed like it was going to explode. I was not prepared for how much my boobs were going to change. So again, my midwife, with her confidence, saved me. She offered conviction, certainty, and strength. Immediately after Jack was born, her words were certain. "Your baby *will* latch. You will figure this out, both of you. It is nature's way." Even in my confidence in what she was saying, I didn't know what to expect.

However, I thought to myself, *Yep, she's right. She's speaking my language. I am part of nature.* Just because we are human does not exclude us from what this Universe is evolving to and the rhythms of nature. But we must relax. Nature isn't worried. So why are we?

Unfortunately, with everything from my boobs growing exponentially to trusting other rhythms (your baby is on their own clock, knows when they should be born and when they should eat, etc.), I don't remember anyone ever sitting me down and saying, "Lona, your body is connected to the rhythms of this world, just like animals. Respect it. Respect everything. There is a natural flow to things. Trust in it." That message over and over again is something I hope I can do for my children.

We all need to hear it, feel it, and trust it until it becomes who we are. To feel so natural and confident in your own beingness from a young age? Wow, that would fix many of our world's issues. It's part of my purpose on earth to help others connect back to this natural potential we all hold.

However, if anything, we are taught the opposite from a young age. Most women are taught to hate their periods instead of honoring them. We just look at it as a nuisance instead of a cycle that helps clean our body and also regulate life on earth. That this cycle is life-giving. I don't remember feeling honored in my sex ed lessons in public school. See the difference? Why are we not given a different narrative to our bodies that truly create miracles? After years of programming that this monthly cycle sucks, all of a sudden, we need to trust it to bring in life and sustain life? Can you see the paradox we have been sold?

Same with our boobs. We are taught they are too small, too big, or meant for sexuality, specifically. We see "perfect," manufactured, and under-the-knife boobs in our daily media. So what nature has granted each of us, and for what reasons, seems to go by the wayside.

We don't talk about breasts as amazing, life-giving producers.

We don't discuss that human milk is specifically gifted with the right antibodies and nutrients for your exact child in the right quantities. No, instead we are given messages that do not honor this learning curve of motherhood. That you are not producing enough, that your baby is lazy, etc. I hate hearing that. Mainly because I wonder if, given more support and different messaging, this would be the case. We have become very disconnected to what has gotten humanity to this current place and time. We *are* nature, not separate from it in our perceived superiority.

Here's the good news. We can change this. I know it's not a black-and-white thing. I know my feelings of lack in this area of my "education" are not felt by every woman. However, I do think we can do better. The shift can come from each of us. Uplift your fellow women. Hold space for pregnant women and new moms. Don't say, "Let me know if you need help." Just go help.

Cook a meal. Hold their baby. Show them how to nurse. Talk to them about birth. Talk to them about their bodies. Talk to them about the absolute gifts their bodies are. Talk to them about the power in their ability to bring life into this world. If we don't taboo these topics and can open a door for communication, it will change everything. It will help women trust themselves again. It will change the way we birth back to a more natural process. We love our babies, no doubt about it, but we don't need to fear them or the process that is unfolding around them.

Women, we can reclaim this power for humanity.

Reflection: What has your learning curve looked like with other women? Who has powerfully held a door open for you? Who has invited you into a sisterhood? It does not have to be someone in your family. If you haven't found someone, would this add more to your life? I know for me it has greatly.

PART III

LESSONS

CHAPTER 28

APPROVE YOURSELF

In entrepreneurship, as in life, there are many experiences that teach. Some feel warm and fuzzy, and some are a school of hard knocks. Some of the learning curves I would not have chosen had I known in advance. However, in hindsight, there was generally invaluable information in these experiences.

One lesson I have witnessed a few times is the higher you grow, the more you stick out, and the more there may be others who don't appreciate your growth. You may never know why they dislike you or what they have against you. Frankly, it's none of your business because it's really not about you. However, for most of us, it feels like a hard lesson to learn when almost everyone is wired to want approval.

This is why having a great support system is helpful. I remember calling one of my consultants to complain about a personal attack, and he point blank said, "Yeah, so what? Keep moving." Okay. I can do that. His confidence helped me find my own.

Another mentor told me once, "Don't want negative feedback? Then stay small. That's the only way to avoid this; if you weren't reaching people, Lona, no one would have a problem with you." Not everyone is going to root for you, nor is anyone designed to have 100 percent of people love them, agree with them, or approve of them. That's okay.

There can and will be amazing people in your corner. There also can be some who once were in your corner and now, for whatever reasons, are not. There are also some who will never be in your camp. That's okay. If you can accept this—the sooner, the better—you will waste less energy. As long as you are in your own corner, you've got something! Many people are directly working against themselves. That will get you nowhere.

These lessons that came under attack, feeling vulnerable or misunderstood, or having to make a hard business decision all grew me. Letting an employee go or taking a metaphorical bullet because someone didn't share my vision made me stronger. Made me more certain that I needed to grow my conviction in the vision I had because I was needed to lead it.

Over time, I became more comfortable with using my voice in the world. I became more comfortable with sharing my vision and not questioning myself as much. It was not cold turkey, overnight that these habits and ways of thinking changed for me. I wanted to be accepted and liked. I wasn't trying to piss people off when I spoke my mind. I was not trying to step on others' toes when we opened more than one practice; I wanted to help more people, and I saw opportunities. I didn't want to piss other allopathic practitioners off when I suggested natural options for patients. But here's the kicker: I control me. I don't control others. I don't control how they receive what I say or do either. This is the lesson we all get to learn. We control ourselves. That's it. So spend more time working on yourself and knowing the depth of who you are before you get hung up on what others are doing, thinking, or saying.

As I realized more of what I just pointed out, I became comfortable speaking from the heart. You can feel it when someone speaks from this place. It's powerful. There is a different tone and energy to their words and message. It generally attracts more people who want to listen as well. I stopped worrying so much about how others were going to receive what I was saying and instead connected to my heart (my purpose, my energy) and spoke what I felt compelled to say.

A mentor said to me as I was nervous to speak at a very large event, "Lona it's not your job to control what the audience receives; you only get to deliver a message. They control what they hear." That perspective has helped me many times over when I am sharing a message at a seminar or even in a one-on-one setting. My job is to speak my truth or what is on my heart.

I will tell you that trying to get approval from everyone is exhausting and, ultimately, will only limit you. Read that again because it's a hard lesson for most of us to swallow.

I will add this too: many times, the people who want to be liked the most and who have a tough time asserting themselves think they are hurting no one by trying to ally and stay friends with everyone. Little do they see that they cut their own growth (hurt themselves) by staying small to fit in all relationships.

When inspiration hits, I have generally found that our problems will come with solutions if we are willing to take them. Rapidly moving with inspiration, for me, has generally worked out best. When I start to second-guess, lose my compass, or look to others to give me permission, that's when momentum slows down. When I start to worry about what others think or if they will like my message, I am allowing fear to block my momentum.

I'll give you an example. I wrote my first book for my profession when I was really new in practice. However, it was fun for me to write, so I got it edited. I didn't know what the hell I was doing. I got a few mentors to read it, and they were gracious enough to endorse it on the cover. Then, I self-published. I had *no* clue what to do with it, but I sent it around the profession, and it got to some influential people. Doors opened. I didn't sit and wallow in small thoughts or fear thoughts like, *Who am I to write this book? Who am I to send it to this person?* We all have those thoughts at times; we just don't have to let them be dominant.

My goal is to take the ideas as they come to me and move with them. Feel what's on my heart and mind and act. Everyone doesn't have to support your decisions, and you don't have to tell everyone your plans. Just start. Make a move. And keep going! Let your inspiration lead you, not your fear of others or your desire to be liked.

> Reflection: Do you continue to look for approval in a place where you will never receive it? Could you give yourself permission to let it go for today? Who is approving of you? Who is rooting for you? Why do we stare at the few people against us instead of the majority who want to see us thrive? Who is your numero uno? Are you in your own corner?
>
> Most importantly, what is on your heart to create or send out to this world? Could you take more action toward this?

CHAPTER 29

ABUNDANCE

Money can be a controversial topic for many. We hear many mixed messages depending on our upbringing over money. I would like to help you simplify your mindset on this topic. Money is energy. It is neither bad nor good. It is just an energy exchange, and you can make it work for you.

Prior to my awakening in 2009, I had a decent relationship with green paper, a.k.a. money. I knew I could work. I was not scared to work hard or put in extra hours; I always felt I could make more money if needed. I wasn't necessarily abundant, but I was not coming from a lack mindset either.

My parents owned a one-hundred-acre Christmas tree farm. My dad and I have differing opinions on how much I actually worked. However, I do recall being in elementary school, having a small Mead notebook (like one-fourth the size of a standard piece of paper), and writing down my hours each week: one hour, three hours, two hours, etc. I got paid two dollars an hour for fertilizing trees. That was my first job.

I am grateful that I learned to work and expend effort. Early on,

I knew I could have things. I would just need to also have effort and not be lazy; the work, production, and effort equated to an exchange. There is not an ounce of my father that bought into a "something for nothing" mentality. Therefore, that trickled down to me.

Right away, as I opened the doors to my practices, I recognized that I had to give to receive. I had to put effort into many aspects to expect them to grow. So I did that, and an influx of abundance came into my life.

I wanted people to have a great experience. I wanted to help them thrive. I wanted to be my best so I could help others better. I wanted to share what I was learning. That was part of what I was exchanging. *My* energy of service to help others, and in turn they would exchange it back to me in the form of monetary payment.

Knowing what you are passionate about and setting up a way to exchange this for money (a.k.a. a business) is a great start to becoming abundant. For me, I am in this world to help others and myself. I am in this world to share truth and vitalism (trusting your body and this intelligence we are born with). These two ideas, helping and sharing loving truth with others, are quite the combo for abundance. A wild exchange of abundant energy is ready for you if you can help a lot of people.

This is also the reason I am writing this book. To reach a wider audience with my message. To help others "get it." To look deeper at life's patterns and what is unfolding for us. The exchange is that in order to read these messages, the book must be paid for. It's just an energy exchange.

Remember energy returns to sender so you cannot outgive the giver. Ever. Your energy will return to you.

Once this energy starts flowing in terms of abundance, the goal is to keep it flowing. We want to keep money moving. Keep the momentum of energy. I didn't want to feel great about money one month and the next month let the energy drop. I wanted to keep it flowing, energy out and energy in.

So I was taught to automate the flow. That meant to automate everything from bills to savings to paying debts so it meticulously happens every week. I don't want the flow to stagnate. Therefore, I don't stagnate in my desire to exchange, create, give, and keep moving my energy and purpose.

You see, the Universe is going to make the exchange even. You treat people poorly, that's what you get back. You don't hold yourself in high regard, that's what you get back. It's really that simple. Again, another mirror the Universe offers you.

The Universe will always balance abundance. So if you are expressing lack in your relationship with money, the Universe will pay you in other ways. Gifts. Compliments. Banana bread. Referrals. You name it. Just to keep the exchange even.

Abundance is available to everyone. The world is waking up to this. First, we must break our addiction to lack. Lack of anything, really. Lack of money. Lack of freedom. Lack of love. Lack of ideas.

Okay, one last thing to say about money for now before we move on. You cannot be a miser if you are going to feel abundant. You must come from a place of respecting your money and other people's money. You want to move it into strategic places so it can work for you.

These concepts apply to everyone. It doesn't matter if you have a nice salaried job, are an entrepreneur, or work hourly part time. Anyone can learn how to move money like this. The concepts will get you ahead, not the amounts.

Reflection: Have you ever thought of money as energy? Where do you flow money well? In what ways do you receive abundance? Where could you learn how to automate money better in your life or reorganize your money monthly or weekly? Can you create better flow?

ENOUGH FOOD FOR TODAY

My first trip to Haiti was a culture shock for sure. I thought I had seen the third world from other travels. However, my experience of the poverty in Haiti was at a different level than I had witnessed previously in other third-world countries. Even the visual of entering the country from the Dominican border made my jaw drop. I could not imagine the poverty that we were driving into. During my first trips to Haiti, I met a Haitian man, Eddie, who assisted our group with translation. Eddie left a profound impression on me.

One night we were eating dinner together at the place we were staying over the border in the Dominican. We had just crossed back from Haiti and were surrounded by prepared food for us. I was about to get a lesson in abundance.

We were talking about Haitian food, and the conversation changed into something much deeper. He explained to me about his day-to-day life and his relationship with food. He said, "When times are good and I know I have enough to eat for the day, I give some of our extra food to my son and tell him to go give it to another person who won't eat that day."

What? I thought. *Did I hear him correctly? If you have enough to eat for one day, you give the rest to others?*

My jaw dropped. His concept of abundance imprinted on me deeply. Abundance was having enough to eat for one day? Just enough for one day. Wow. Wow. Wow. This conversation seared into my soul.

I was flabbergasted at the juxtaposition of my concept of abundance versus his. I felt uncomfortable and humbled as I realized how much I took for granted and how much I didn't realize the unbelievable amount of abundance I experienced in my life. I also realized we all have so many immense blessings and opportunities to give.

This is part of why I love traveling so much; it changes you. Your state changes. Your world opens up. Seeing other cultures, connecting with humans who are very similar to you and yet live extremely different realities. Knowing others, in a place you never knew existed, changes your view on life.

CHAPTER 30

CONTRAST

After the first five years of business, things were evolving very quickly for me. I was taking learning opportunities left and right. Formal and informal. Seminars, travel, philosophy, business, money, and leadership. Learning about how to lead better. Learning how to communicate (with everyone) more effectively. There were some crash courses in all of those moments.

In my new mindset, there was and is still a part of me that wants everyone and everything to line up perfectly and for "love and light" only to be present. Rainbows too. However, in this bubble or dream I forget how important contrast can be.

Contrast is generally felt as negativity, a hard experience, haters, or anything that challenges you. Contrast is always offering valuable lessons and also delineating more of what you actually want. (For the record, another great resource and mentor I love is Esther Hicks. Her teachings address contrast often.)

It was at this time, about five years into business, right after I found out that I was pregnant with Jack, that my landlord started to play some games. We had about 1,000 square feet for our main practice space. The landlord asked me if I would like to have the other side of the space because the current tenant would not be renewing.

I asked about square footage and if I could get the floor plan and walk through that suite so I could do some mental logistics of what we would do with the space and the buildout necessary.

They told me I had one day and that rent would be the same as what I was paying since it was about the same size space. I took the very limited twenty-four hours and decided yes. Yes, I would like the space. Yes, I was ready to double our size.

I called them, and they told me that they might not have it available, that they might negotiate with the current tenant, who wanted a price break.

I wasn't blind. I knew I was paying more rent (and had been for years) than the other side of the space (for the same square footage). I also had helped them fill that space several times with various other holistic businesses. It was time to put my foot down. I was sick of being jerked around and then paying higher rent.

I knew the building was for sale, and this was the nudge from the Universe I needed. I called the listing number for the property. It was time to look. I had no prior dream of owning real estate. I had no knowledge of owning real estate. However, my bank, my husband, my dad, the realtor, and a couple of close mentors helped me to see the bright side of this and encouraged me to review the offer.

The hard part was that even with those teams of people stacked to back me up, I still had to do something hard. I had to "kick" out the other tenant who didn't have a long-term lease and was month to month so we could expand into the space.

This proved not only difficult in my mind but also difficult to take action towards I received some negative mojo in the process. They were obviously not impressed with me. However, I think I was being tested, and then strengthened. It was not personal. This was business. It was my reason for buying the building—to have more space.

I knew I did want the space. I knew my dream to grow and have things laid out better for our business. There is also a part of me that knows that just because something feels hard doesn't mean it's the wrong decision.

How many of us have stayed in a bad relationship longer than we should? I know I have. How many of us have not moved on from a job or let someone go because we don't want to upset the other person or deal with the consequences, even if it means a happier life in the long run? I know I have. This is rampant in our society. People do *not* go after what would be best for themselves because they think it's selfish or too much to ask, or they are scared to take the steps.

I have found that although at times doing this is going to require some tough experiences, if it's in alignment for you, it will be for others involved, too. The sun comes out after the clouds.

After deciding I was going to make the move, buy the building, and expand, I had to jump through the hoops to make this happen in mid-pregnancy.

I also knew my intentions were good. I want the best for myself, as I do others. I wholeheartedly believe that if I am grounded and making sound decisions for myself, my health, my business, and my relationships, all parties will benefit in the long run. Even if, in the moment, the other person does not feel the same way, things will fall into place.

* * *

It was no surprise that literally in the months after making the building sale and starting our renovations, we had some of the biggest months in practice I had ever had, to date. My team was excited about the expansion. So were our clients. The energy was right.

As we took over the space, I was a brand-new mom and learning how to balance the changes. Energy was pouring out, and energy was coming in. It was a great lesson for me: stepping into my vision and remembering it's not *all* going to smell like roses or be perfect timing in my mind, but there can still be sweetness. Contrast can move you to action. In my case, it had pushed me to take a leap into commercial real estate. I am grateful it did.

Contrast is a great teacher. Feeling negative emotions or having things happen you wish you could change sucks in the moment, but there are always lessons and experiences to grow from in the midst of the contrast. Life offers us many ways to change and grow; contrast is a great motivator to seek out a different option.

Reflection: What is contrasting in your life right now? What does not seem to be lining up? What sucks? What is de-energizing? What is pissing you off? Is there something you could do to see the contrast and then make a change to make your life better?

TO DECIDE OR NOT TO DECIDE

In reality, almost any decision we make or don't make affects others connected to us. We may not see just how dramatically it impacts them. That's a good way to put things in perspective. You can spin out decisions (or lack of decisions) and think about how they affect others. Do you see how I included lack of decisions in the previous sentence? Not making a decision is making a choice. Read that again. If you are a passive person, you are still making decisions and choices with your silence or inaction. Ripples of energy follow these quiet decisions or a lack of decision. This is a reminder for you.

PART IV

MOMMING

CHAPTER 31

CONSTANT MOTION

In 2015, about five to six years into practice, I was working in Chippewa Falls and Hudson, at both practices. I was lucky enough that my mom agreed to watch Jack on the days I was in her area. We were in the thick of life and making things work. We were constantly in motion, but it was working.

I got to be home with Jack one to two days a week. Jack and I were making the commute two days a week and sleeping at my parents' house one night a week to do less driving. Kyle's business was still going well in Minneapolis, and life had a weird balance, but overall things "worked." Kyle and I still had very separate lives most weeks, but we now shared a common bond of our new baby boy.

When Jack was about six months old, we took him on a service trip to Jamaica and then came back for a week and then went down to St. Lucia for my brother's wedding. We had the traveling babe. It felt like a great start to the year. Little did I know what 2016 had in store for us.

We all were living this new dream. Our new roles and routines with our son. Our new ways of being and creating balance in the world. Kyle and I balancing businesses and home life. My mom and dad helped me with Jack, and I had a great team at work that had allowed me to cut my hours back to three days a week at one practice and a half day at the other.

There was new, uncharted territory. I was traveling for work almost monthly (speaking at events) and bringing a baby in tow. Luckily, most of the time, this was pretty easy because my profession is so warm to organic lifestyles.

Toting a baby to a conference where I was going to speak and nurse throughout the conference was pretty normal in our circles. Flying with a baby who is nursing is also not a huge deal. The hardest part is just how to carry him and bring what you need for the trip, suitcase, and car seat in the airport. An extra hand would be great at times. Many times, I traveled with my work team, or at least one or two of them, so I usually had help.

I loved having him with me everywhere. It was also a valid excuse to become more introverted. Declining late nights felt normal. It also was survival to get any sleep possible. For the first time in my life, my new routines were centered around someone else. It felt good. I was loving "momming."

There was still every other weekend where Kyle would drive and be gone for five to six hours on Friday and Sunday, picking up the girls, and those weekends had a different cadence from the rest of our life. This, for the most part, was working.

There were moments where I lost my shit in trying to balance it all. So I am not trying to say it was roses 24/7. For instance, one moment that stands out in my mind that was ugly was when

Jack was a few days old and Kyle was already back to work and left for an evening to go to a T-ball game that was three hours away. I felt really alone and really pissed that he left.

Hormones probably played a role, but I didn't know how to handle them in the moment and was angry, sad, and overwhelmed all at once. And unlike my mother, who I never saw fight, I let him know it. That fight will forever stand out in my head of how enraged I was that he left.

However, for the most part, this new light in our life, a common bond, and a different lens to see the world had opened up more for both of us. There was more commonality in our marriage and more sense of unity between us and the life we were living.

We no longer were two completely separate circles living in the same house. Previously, my circle had encompassed my priorities, vision, and passions, and his circle had encompassed his own. Finding mutual ground had been tough. Especially as I had given up partying, which used to be an activity we both were good with. Now, with Jack, we had a little healthier overlap.

With the beginning of 2016, we were traveling as a family more. We were home more overall. My identity was changing from who I was before becoming a mom, and oddly, I felt really good about that. I had willingly stepped into this new identity.

Of course, I had new routines too. I still *loved* my role as an entrepreneur and chiropractor. I also adored my new role as a mom. Even being married was starting to feel more "normal." The first year of marriage, I would cringe when we used our married words. "Wife" or "husband." They didn't seem real. I don't know where that response came from, but for some reason, it was hard for me to make those words fit.

That part of me was starting to change. I was learning how to live life not just for numero uno. Marriage was my crash course. Motherhood felt more natural for sure. Both Kyle and Jack (and now I am sure my new babe growing in my belly as I write this) have been and will be amazing teachers and catalysts for metamorphosis in my life.

> Reflection: Have you had a period of your life where things were moving fast? Where you barely could come up for air? How did you stay grounded? How long was it sustainable?

CHAPTER 32

FIND AN EASIER WAY

Up until this time, since we had gotten married, we had lived about an hour away from my practice, and both of us were still commuting long hours to work. Both of my practices were running. I had a great team and business partner to balance both businesses, and things were working.

I was becoming exhausted with the drive and not getting home until eight o'clock or later each night. Then, co-sleeping and nursing every night, which was not something I was willing to change. Some nights I would stay at my parents' house to break up having to drive. It was not a sustainable plan. Which meant something else had to change.

We had almost no family time during the week. Kyle left very early in the morning as I was waking up, and I would get home four to five hours after he was done with work at night. Again, we ran very independent lives during the week; it was starting to become apparent that this "way" of living was not going to work long term.

I felt pretty alone parenting during the week and some weekends also. I was tired from breastfeeding at night (all night sometimes), driving long days during the week and breastfeeding during lunch, and then picking him up at night and getting home late. I finally went to Kyle and said, "Something has to change. I can't live here anymore."

We had been loosely talking about making a move eventually to be closer to my original practice and my parents. However, now I knew this had to happen sooner than later. I am sure many new moms can relate to the feelings I had.

Kyle eventually agreed we could rent a house in my hometown near the practice for the winter and keep up two places before we made any other decision. I was grateful.

We decided to buy a house back in my hometown. We closed on it in May 2016. Within six months of establishing the house, Kyle decided to move there (so we were not living in two cities) and start a much longer commute himself.

I felt a bit guilty that he had to drive a lot or figure out a new working situation in the area, but I was just grateful that my long days with a baby would be easier.

We also lived three miles away from my parents; again, something I never thought I would have advocated for. It ended up being a huge blessing, as my dad ended up needing a lot of help and support for what was to come. We also had the blessing of having helping hands closer for Jack!

Many changes have occurred since this point where I recognized my breaking point and decided I had to do something different. It was time to look for an easier or better path for the long run.

We now both work in the same area and have evenings together; family time has definitely improved. It took work, some hard steps, and a willingness to change rather than throw in the towel.

For us, 2016 was a year of transitions. We knew what we were doing needed to change for the longevity of our family. We found an easier way.

Reflection: What have you gone through that, in hindsight, you are amazed at your ability and resilience to get through? Long days? A tough grind? Something else? What was it preparing you for? Did it make you hard or create more adaptability and soften you? Could you find an easier way?

CHAPTER 33

PERPETUALLY COVERED IN MILK

It was this summer of 2016 that so much had settled in. We had our new house in Chippewa Falls. Jack was one. "Momming" was my new favorite everything. Kyle and I were starting to domesticate ourselves better and figure out this new life in a new location.

I was still breastfeeding Jack. First, that had started with me just wanting him to latch and take things day by day, which is probably good advice to any new mom. I had my warrior-woman midwife (with a gentle soul) who instilled confidence in me that not only could I birth, but my baby would latch, my milk would come in, and we would settle into a rhythm. She was right.

Next, I wanted to make it to six months of breastfeeding. Then, twelve months. Then I read about child-led weaning and nursing in other cultures. Okay, we were in this for the long haul. It's natural, but for most of us it still feels foreign. To talk about a baby nursing or see a baby nursing (as a toddler or older) is still not that "normal" in our Western society.

In my opinion, we need to normalize these conversations between women and do what my midwife did for me. She talked me through it as much as she could and assured me it was normal, I would heal, and things were right on track. If it were not for her, I wouldn't have had anyone I felt would hold the door for me to lean on in this accelerated learning curve. As much as my own mom was available, she didn't talk much about any of it.

I will also say this: it's damn good you have all those oxytocin love hormones that bind you to your child. This bond is what allows you to basically hand over your body for the period of time you will breastfeed. It's beautiful and like nothing else I had known. Your body is not your own during this time. It's also comfort. A buffet and the most stable home for your baby.

I include this part because it is healing for me to write about my learning curve of awakening, adulthood, and what has left the biggest imprints on me. Years of breastfeeding and the evolution of becoming a mother—whew. It showed me a lot of what I was embracing in my evolution of natural healing.

In our core, we are animals. We have innate knowledge in our DNA of how to do some of these things that are biologically imperative. It is our culture that sometimes can interrupt this pattern of nature, and the more we can be supported by women who can help us embrace some of this inborn knowledge, I think the better it is for everyone.

Our men, too, need to embrace these messages and their own inborn nature. To be strong, supportive, and engaged partners in the birth process and what comes after is a gift we can help our little boys step into for future generations.

If birthing a full human (that you had no "education" to make) didn't convince you of the Intelligence that is present in every shred of this Universe, then you get another jaw-dropping experience with breastfeeding to help confirm that. Breastmilk is like God's plan to grow your new gift. It also heals both mom and baby and prepares them to grow into their next phases of life.

The other thing I think it did for me is *bind* me so strongly to this child. It was like if he moved, I knew it. We co-slept because I couldn't think about not being in the same room as him. To me, this is also a tactic of survival of the fittest. If he was going to need to nurse a couple of times a night or sometimes all night long, then I was going to do it half asleep. Then we both could be happy.

The thought of actually getting out of bed and going to a different room to sit up, put him back to sleep, and then do it all again thirty minutes later seemed impossible.

Everyone strikes their own balance, so breastfeeding and co-sleeping conversations are not meant to shame anyone who thinks differently or does it differently. It was merely part of my hippy, natural, "granola" learning curve of what has taught me to trust this body, trust this Universe, and celebrate the true miracles around every curve of the adventure.

I do think about how grateful I am that I had my children after my wake-up call. Prior to it, my mind was not ready to honor and trust this natural part of myself. I had many layers to peel back before I could rest in these natural ways of letting life unfold. I had never been someone to run to the medical doctor, but also, I didn't realize how much our body, mind, and spirit can show us what it needs and what it doesn't if we just listen.

This is also my purpose for writing this. I hope I inspire some of you to go back to your instincts and intuition if you have left them by the wayside.

The adventures of the first year of life are thick with miracles. From your baby growing and growing and growing to all the changes your body goes back through and the fact that it keeps nourishing this human who is changing every day is simply miraculous.

There were times when I really wanted Kyle to do more (help at night), but the reality was I didn't give him much chance. Then there were times when I felt bad for him. The baby needs their mom constantly (who has the goods: boobs and milk). If dad had those, the baby would be attached to him, and mom would be the extra wheel. I just remember thinking, *I am so glad to be his mom because I would be jealous if I didn't get to hold him and take care of him this much.*

So my heart goes out to new dads too. It's a whole new way of life for them regardless of feeding circumstances. There are new dynamics for the whole family. That's for sure.

During the day, besides reducing my clinic/patient hours I had the awareness I would not get this time back. So I reduced how much time I was spending working with other chiros and also cut back travel some. The previous two years, I had helped handfuls of others with their startup processes, mentoring them. It was time for me to step back some of what I was doing, and for the first time, I felt okay with that. All part of my transformation in becoming a mom.

For the most part, from Jack's needs and working/running businesses, the concept of free time had vaporized. However, we were all figuring it out. I still, most days, was finding twenty minutes to walk or run, and life was good. For the moment, things had a nice, new cadence.

Reflection: How in tune with your instincts do you feel? Do you follow your intuition? Can you resonate with the fact that you are part of the natural world and its rhythms? How could you honor that more in your life, in your family, or with your body?

CHAPTER 34

LIFE UPSIDE DOWN

I remember sitting on the grass that autumn in my parents' yard. Just as Jack's birth is etched into my head, so is this moment with my mom. It marks the beginning of a very tragic time for us.

My mom had started acting a little funny that summer. She had helped my grandma, who was in her mid-nineties, clean out her childhood house and move into an assisted living apartment. My dad and I knew she was stressed and wasn't sleeping well.

She was post-cancer by a couple of years. She had been taking my grandma to her medical appointments. My grandmother, a very kind soul, was also a very quiet woman. Never one to put herself first, and it was always hard to get her to say much.

My grandmother had started to complain about one of her eyes and her sight. So after a couple of weeks, my mom got an appointment for my grandmother to visit an eye doctor. My mom took her to an appointment for her eyes, and at the appointment, the doctor told my mother, "If you had brought her here two weeks ago, I could have saved the sight in this eye."

What a wonderful comment. (Can you sense my sarcasm?) My mother was not legally responsible for my grandmother, and also not responsible for her medically. She was helping her. She hadn't known how bad the eye was because my grandmother did not say much.

However, she took this comment to heart. Words are challenging because we never know how others process them or if we receive their meanings as intended. I think my mother took this guilt to heart.

After that, there was a deluge of related comments from my mother about how guilty she felt about not taking good care of my grandma. Her guilt seemed to consume her, and she started to lose touch with the reality the rest of us saw.

My dad and I were flabbergasted. We didn't know what to say to her to help her see the situation differently. She had been helping my grandma with almost everything.

She helped go through her mail weekly. She helped her make sure her coumadin levels were okay for her blood and helped organize her weekly pills. She also grocery shopped for her. However, none of that help seemed to matter. The fact that my grandma had lost her sight seemed to be a tipping point for what my mother could handle.

So the memory that is etched in my head is a beautiful fall day. I am looking at my beautiful sixty-one-year-old mother, sitting in the grass that day, and she looked so sad. So broken. Her shoulders were slumped. She was sitting on the ground with her long legs to the side of her, folded. I had never seen my mom sit like this—like a child, defeated.

I felt helpless too. I just wanted to make her understand. I am not sure how many times we all had conversations with her, telling her, "You didn't do anything wrong." We had tried to help her process her responsibility and guilt over a hundred times. My mom seemed incapable of trusting anything other than that she had failed.

She kept saying how terrible she was. She kept commenting on how bad it was that she didn't take better care of grandma and that she had made all these terrible decisions for my grandmother's health. My dad and I just kept exchanging looks, not knowing what was happening.

In the next coming weeks, our lives were going to be radically altered. It's hard for me to even write some of this because the experience was so horrifying to me. My mom started to very quickly lose grasp of any reality that my dad and I were witnessing. She blamed herself entirely for my grandmother's decline. We tried to rationalize with her. We tried to help her see that her mother was just getting very old. We also wanted to make sure she remembered it was *not* her responsibility to do everything for her mom.

My mom couldn't hear it. Over and over, she repeated how bad she was. She became afraid of everything. It was like watching a train wreck. Her decline happened so fast. It felt like her thought pattern and ability to grasp the reality that most of us were living changed in several days.

She stopped eating. Anything. She didn't leave her room. She stopped responding to our questions. If we tried to push her to answer some of our questions, like about what she was thinking or if she would like to get some help, she would lash out.

Ugly, ugly words my mother had never said before to me (or probably anyone) were hurled at me and my dad frequently. If you tried to push her to do anything, she would lash out. The hurt she was feeling was easy to see because she used violent words if she was not left alone. It felt like she wanted to die.

This lashing out when we would try to help her made her seem like a caged animal full of fear. Even her eyes were different. I didn't know if it was because she spent almost all day in a dark room or something more fundamental was gone in her.

In all that I had seen thus far in human behavior and human health (in practice, life, and school), I was not equipped to handle this. I had *very* little awareness of what to say, do, or think about what I was witnessing in my mom.

She stayed in her bed in the dark and didn't leave except to go to the bathroom. Her outbursts were scary; I didn't recognize her. She refused food and any help or discussion of help. There seemed to be no ounce of love for anyone left in her.

My dad asked me to check on her a couple of evenings he was gone. The lights were totally shut off in the house. Driving up, the house was completely dark, and on the dark one-hundred-acre farm, I felt fear. I had asked Kyle to go with me because I was afraid to walk into my childhood house in the dark. I didn't trust my mom.

In this stage, she seemed capable of anything. Hurting me. Hurting herself. I was scared each time I would go over there that I would find her dead. Maybe my mind was playing tricks on me, but I didn't know what to expect. I knew my dad had these thoughts too.

It all seemed too surreal and horrifying to process, and it was going to get worse. My beautiful soft-spoken mom, who didn't get up in the morning without putting herself together for the day, felt like a scary monster to me. It's hard for me to even write that because I miss her so much.

This started in early fall of 2016. My parents own a Christmas tree farm, so by the time Thanksgiving and tree season had come, we were in a bad place. She was living in her room 100 percent of the time. She hadn't eaten in well over a month and a half and was barely drinking water. It was like watching a passive suicide. For the record, I think subconsciously that is what we were witnessing.

We had gotten her to go to the hospital, fighting literally physically against us the whole way, twice. Once there, she would somehow pull herself together and decline treatment, and the hospital had no choice but to let her go. It was a waste. By this point she had dropped thirty-five pounds. She was the skinniest I had ever witnessed. Her hair was getting shaggy (again, a woman who always was put together to the nines), and she hadn't showered in many weeks.

It felt like life had dropped us totally upside down. We didn't know how to help. I had never been to this place before where life internally and externally felt totally foreign to me. I had never felt abandoned, fear, grief, disbelief, or my roots shaken like this.

My dad and I were horrified by what we were witnessing and our lack of ability to help in any way. My mom had no history of mental health issues. No history of this type of behavior. My mom was the person who was always calm and collected. She was *always* put together.

I always felt somewhat inadequate as her daughter, like I was a bull in a china shop compared to her. I would joke (but be serious) that she wanted a daughter who was more put together, more feminine, so to see her this way felt like the world had dumped itself upside down.

I share this story because I know I am not the only person who goes through very intense periods of devastation, or holy-shit-what's-happening moments where life is flipped upside down and has to learn how to keep moving as well as process what's happening.

Reflection: Have you had a point in life where you felt you were stripped naked? Or you felt guttural emotions and fears you didn't even know you could have playing out? It is humbling and can feel really difficult to acknowledge what is still good in your life. Could you find the good that was still there?

CHAPTER 35

WHITE KNUCKLING

Part of the challenge for me personally during that time was I still was running multiple businesses and seeing patients. Jack was a little over one year of age, and I had to scramble to find a new daycare situation for him early in the fall, as things had started to decline so fast at my mom's.

My dad was trying to hold their business together. Meanwhile, he was watching his partner of many decades decline and lose touch with our experience of reality. It felt like she hated us. I really think now that she just hated that we wouldn't leave her alone to die.

As my dad struggled to process, there were quite a few days he would show up, sometimes at six o-clock in the morning as I was starting my day (still nursing through the night), and unload some of his worry and stress about what we could do to help Mom or what had happened that night before with her. I don't blame him. I would have done the same, probably. We both were white knuckling each day, and it seemed like a nightmare that we kept waking up to.

It was like the two of us were the only people who, week by week, saw what was happening. My brother lived out of state, so he was involved by phone, but it was different.

By Christmas, we felt we had exhausted all of our abilities to try to help her or get her to help without intervention. Finally, one of our family MDs came to the house and helped us get the county involved to get her to a treatment facility and see if they could help her.

I would like to say this story ends better. I'll make it short. Over the next six months, my mom was in moved into two mental health hospital wings and eventually a long-term mental health institution. The only improvement that seemed to occur after several months in these places is that she would eat a small amount. I shouldn't undercredit this because that was a big step. We didn't fear her passive suicide once she started eating a bit. However, nothing seemed to help the fact that she seemed to have lost the desire to live.

I felt like I was living the Twilight Zone, visiting my mom where she was basically locked up, with my one-year-old. Hearing others in her unit with severe mental challenges uttering things as we visited. Seeing the life missing in her eyes and in the eyes of almost everyone we saw in those facilities. It was, again, horrifying. I wanted to stick my head in the sand and pretend none of this was real. It didn't seem like it could be. In my mind, my pretty, soft-spoken mother who spent three decades teaching science to middle-schoolers should not have been there.

My dad drove to the facilities every day, sometimes two times a day, and it was an hour each way. His commitment to her was amazing. I went weekly, usually. We would sit with her. Sometimes playing cards. I do think she was happy we came, but it was so hard to tell because she did nothing to care for herself.

For me, one of the hardest parts was that very few people around me could understand what my family and I were going through. It's hard to explain this tragedy to people, especially if they knew my mom before or don't have a lot of context for mental health. Also, I didn't want to articulate any of it; it was hard to understand myself.

Others who were close wanted to know how she was doing. Having to give updates was exhausting. Also, it was difficult to figure out what to say—I am sure for all of us. Most of all, it was sad. Sad to watch her and try to understand her. Really sad to think about what she was feeling and thinking, and very sad for my dad. Sad for me. Sad for many.

I learned also it's hard to explain to someone who has never lived through something gut-wrenching or has no experience with the challenges of mental health. It made me realize who could really offer me some grace and compassion and who could not.

It also made me realize how I had lacked so much empathy in the past for some of the difficult times people were experiencing and walking through. I have realized that, though we don't walk in the same shoes, tragedy and challenge open up empathy and compassion for others' situations and the realization that life is so precious, joyful, and equally heartbreaking.

It was like I was being gutted and cracked open through this experience. To have more empathy and more compassion for people whether we knew what was happening with them or not.

I had never had my roots shaken so hard. Driving to visit her in the institution showed me the fragility of life and how quickly things can change. The daughter in me was crushed. I still feel this (though less often), and it has showed me new context.

What really matters at the core of me? These deeper questions and deeper levels of awareness I really couldn't even begin to understand before because I had no context. Nothing had felt ripped from me before; nothing also had felt so completely unfair before. My mom had already gone through quite a bit in the past few years. It felt hard to know how to process what was happening then. It was a radical period of learning how to survive, not sink, and consciously look for what I was still grateful for. I would snuggle my baby boy and try to put my energy in this new being.

Reflection: In great struggle, have you found a silver lining? Have you been able to find small or big gratitude to focus on so your mind doesn't sink into despair?

CHAPTER 36

SILVER LININGS

As of 2020, my mother is still alive, thankfully. She is at home now and has been for most of the last three years. She is much more mentally aware now; however, it's like she is a battery that only physically charges to 2 percent. Some days are better days. I can have a good conversation with her, or she will send me texts. She barely leaves her room and some days does not seem very interested in much. (As I write this in 2020, she hasn't left the house in months, and it's not due to COVID-19.)

My dad is her caretaker. We have tried so many avenues of ideas with her that could potentially offer help; she shuts them all down. She has missed every holiday (with the exception of us coming to her) since this has happened. The weirdest part is that it is like we are grieving someone who is still alive. Yet still trying to hold on to hope and not get swallowed by what is.

There is much sadness, and I could continue to share about what I have experienced since 2016 and the fast and then slow disintegration of what I knew and had come to expect of my birth family. However, this book is not meant to be that type of book.

However, it *is* a book about awareness and finding *life*. A fuller *life*. So how has this gut-wrenching experience given me life?

Actually, it has in many ways. When I can get out of being the "daughter" and move further back in my perspective, I can see different gifts in this experience. I try to get a bird's-eye view on the situation so I can see openings.

The first is I learned how to empathize and hold space. My mom showed me what it was like to feel deep pain of my own, and I could see the deep pain my mom's experience, though I can't understand it. Each of my family members has their own trauma and pain from this.

Seeing and feeling the underbelly of life and human emotion changes your awareness. The brokenness, the heartache, the suffering—it's all part of life at times, part of the human experience. We can't just see the world through a Pollyanna lens 100 percent of the time. We all are walking around having this human component of an array of experiences and an array of surprises in how life unfolds.

Learning to honor that things can be a blessing even when they feel guttural and certainly unplanned. Allowing some space for whatever is unfolding and not avoiding anything that feels heavy—that way it doesn't swallow you unannounced. Avoiding or pretending the darker aspects of life do not exist is not my suggestion. My suggestion is to see it, don't avoid it, and consciously choose to still write your own story and take actions to ensure this.

There were days I did well with life during this time. I felt immense gratitude for other aspects of my life. There were days when I just wanted to curl into a ball and go snuggle my mom and cry. I wanted to curl up and say, "I give up because you give up." I wanted to be angry, sad, and scared all at the same time and have her fix it. I didn't let myself linger too long in those thoughts.

I wanted to say, "This isn't fair. You are supposed to be my mom and supposed to be a doting grandma." I let myself have my self-pity and sadness. Then there were more days my heart just broke for her brokenness and for my dad's commitment. Witnessing their breakdown. It still gets me, and I cry writing this paragraph.

It also really put things into perspective. You never know what people's public life is compared to their private life. During 2016, I won an "entrepreneur of the year" award from our local county at a big business breakfast with Darryl Worley (the country singer), as the main event. He played "I Miss My Friend," and I watched my dad cry at the table. He had come to celebrate the award with us. Ugh. Heavy.

It was such a juxtaposition to accept this award with my team and then know that the thing that would actually make my day was if my mom would just start taking showers so she could go home from the mental health institution. Again, you may think you know someone, but you don't know what their experience is. I try to keep a better perspective on that. I really try to learn how to read where people are, as well as honor the fact that I only know a sliver about anyone's experience.

My husband did an excellent job of holding space for me—keeping things "normalish" at home and letting me have the space I needed to process. This ordeal helped me unify further in my marriage. He didn't talk about my mom if I didn't, yet if I wanted to talk, he would. He didn't seem to judge her or me. That I appreciated. I was sick of hearing what people thought of her situation. Or about me and my dad and what we should do.

The breakdown of my childhood family unit forced me into identifying more with my future family unit that had already started with Jack but still had many jagged edges. Through all of this, we were starting to integrate more. It was a silver lining.

Reflection: Where have you found a blessing hidden among grief or a challenge? Have you looked for it? There are silver linings to be found. What has helped you through some of the most challenging periods of your life?

THE PRACTICE OF MEDITATION

Now I meditate first thing in the morning, many times for only five minutes. I think most people are afraid to try meditation more than a couple of times because they are frustrated that their minds continue to "think." We all do that.

The practice of meditation is just that: a practice. Use your breath, a phrase or word (a mantra—I took transcendental meditation, so that's the technique I usually use), or a guided meditation, and allow yourself to keep coming back to this in your mind. Unwanted thought? Let it go, and come back to the center point, breath or mantra. Next unwanted thought? Let it go; come back to the center. It becomes relaxing and helpful the more often you practice.

Clearing the mind, whether through running, meditation, laughing, snuggling, or anything that helps you release, is calming, helps access higher states (meaning you go from frustration to neutrality or an analytical mind to a peaceful mind), and is a great time afterward to start to dream.

As I have paid attention more and asked myself better questions, life doesn't have to feel so rough. Now, an idea will pop in while I am running or meditating or really anytime (while in a good state), and I pay attention to it.

Some thoughts we have are fear thoughts. Some thoughts we have are truly inspired. You get to choose which ones you follow as your truth. Fear isn't all bad. It helps lead us to safety when we need it. The trouble is that some of us stay too safe for too long.

Having a practice like meditation can help immensely when going through tough times.

JUST LOVE ME

I wouldn't wish my mom's experience or our family's struggle on my worst enemy. However, the unconditional love I have learned as I have tried to process this is a gift. And the awareness of my sadness, anger, and disbelief has been a learning curve I have grown from. My mom has maintained through this that what she needs from us is *love*.

Love. That's it. When we ask her how we should respond or what we could or should do to try to help her, she says, "Just love me."

It's interesting that we want to *do* more for her but when asked to just *love*, that feels unacceptable. That *love* couldn't be enough; we must *do* more. In the last year, I have settled into thinking that maybe, just maybe, we should all just listen to her. Love her. Stop asking her to be different. Not expect anything to change and just support her and also ourselves. Do what we need to do for ourselves. That is loving too.

My new perspective is learning that just because life doesn't turn out as the Cinderella story doesn't mean that it isn't perfection. Her resolve is somewhat ridiculous. She maintains just "love me" as she declines anything else that could be an option to help her.

My dad and I are doers. We want to save her. We want her to be involved again and have a life that we want her to have. However, we both know that she ultimately holds that key. So love and acceptance are the job for us to undertake if we are willing.

I am also coming to terms with her teaching us something far greater by her life being in this state. She may be a canary in the coal mine for so many lessons right now. Perhaps I will be able to share more on this later. For now, I think it's a lesson in unconditional love.

PART V

ALIGNMENT

CHAPTER 37

REGROUPING

As I have mentioned, I have a deep philosophy and faith with my new life view (since I awakened to it and began learning more in 2009). As life continues to happen, I have only trusted and learned to double down in this philosophy. As I have learned to witness my own patterns (some that are healing and others I am avoiding), and as I have gotten to witness others' journeys of awareness and healing, I can see this view on life unfolding.

Learning to see synchronicities in life and learning how to manage my own state has created immense blessings in life. That doesn't mean that I think I see it all. Far from it. However, it becomes easier to see the interconnections as you view life this way. It really is like magic. When you "mess" up, you can regroup faster.

Awareness and healing are an inside-out job, and we don't get to see how these shifts look before we make them. For some, healing will create more ease. For others, there is going to be immense discomfort, and that is *still* healing. This is why it's so important to realize we only control ourselves.

Holding space for myself and others to heal and experience life (from this inside-out perspective) is why I am writing this book and why I love going to work. It is also why I see that just because someone is living in a state of "dis-ease" doesn't mean they are always ready to regroup or change what has gotten them to that point.

A great friend of mine said, in a podcast interview, something that really struck a chord with me. Dr. Wade said, "The doctor of the future is the patient." This is a spin-off of the quote from Thomas Edison, who said, "The doctor of the future will give no medicine but will interest his patient in the care of the human frame, in diet and in the cause and prevention of disease."

You (no matter your background) are your own best doctor. You are in control of your state, and your state determines everything. Your body, your life, your abundance. What are you tuning to; what are you being a conduit for? Is it easeful and loving? Or is it chaotic, dis-eased, and inflexible. If you don't like it, how are you shifting or regrouping to create something new?

We have forgotten, too, that the body is not all we are. In chiropractic, we use the term "triune" to describe life's connections between mind, body, and spirit, or our terms of matter, force, and intelligence. Basically, what I want to emphasize is the body is not separate from these other aspects. The physical body is in relationship with our mind/mental pattern and emotions, the energy that we carry, and its connection to something bigger.

We are not silos. Things don't fit neatly in one area, though modern healthcare seems to want to organize us that way. Our spirituality is not in the kitchen while our mental health is in the basement and our body in the bedroom. The whole house must be explored and acknowledged.

These aspects to us are always communicating. This is why when we have a lack of harmony in our belief systems, our thought patterns will show up in the body. When we treat our body (on the inside) with disrespect—feeding it poor food, poor thoughts, or poor fluids, or no movement—of course it's going to reap what was sown.

To not teach people the power they hold for their own health, well-being, and vibrant life is one of the biggest disservices to humanity. That is my reason for writing this book. To showcase my learning curve in recognizing my own power and reclaiming it. Recognizing my own strength in mind, body, and spirit.

As we learn this, it is easier to see when we are needing to regroup. To change our state or to put our own oxygen mask on first before anything else can occur. Sometimes we forget this order. "I want to help you, but I am not in a good state." It does not work that way. Oxygen mask for self, first, before others. Regroup for yourself first; then help others.

I'll give you some examples.

One night, after about forty-eight hours of watching my Facebook feed and reading too much about the powers that be (and may be crashing down) in our system (control of the media, politics, financial system, and medical cartel, for example), I was in a freaked-out state. Two nights in a row I had read too much of this right before bed.

This left me uneasy and uncomfortable. I felt I could not just sit and meditate—I wanted to know what I could do. I wanted to know the actions to take to help others wake up to some of the corruption that we are being sold and see how we give our power away. Frustration was the emotion I was registering.

Also, I was not in my normal glass-half-full place. I had started the previous mornings writing the chapters on my mom, which had me feeling sadness. You can see how these states start the snowball.

So after two days of Facebook, stress about the state of affairs, and emotions about my mom, I argued with Kyle. Jack told us both to not use swear words (Mom of the year), and then he lost his new race car toy, so we spent an hour looking for it; he went to bed crying and much too late. I could feel in my own body the day was an off day; stress was present even if it was just small things. I needed to regroup and change my state. A pause and a reset.

As I was lying there snuggling him, I told myself, *Lona, breathe. Relax your tension. All is well.* I thought about how grateful I was that Jack was snuggling me and that I knew we would find his car. Literally one minute later, Kyle came into the room and had found the race car. Jack fell asleep moments later.

Now some of you may say, "So what? You found a little lost car!" However, I don't look at situations like anything is random anymore. The car (for which we had looked for over an hour) was found literally one minute after I relaxed my state.

You may think I am a whack job, but you have read this far, so probably not. These are no longer coincidences to me. The car shows up when the energy shifts. This shows the power we hold in creating our outer world through the inside-out process. We are mirrors. When we are in chaotic states, we create more chaos. Division. Rough energy. Nothing seems "right."

When we remember our power and reclaim our state and energy, life shifts; it's magic.

Another example: in 2018, I really thought my mom was going to show up for Thanksgiving at our house. She kept saying she would try to come. The daughter in me continued to hope she meant that. Now keep in mind, she had not come to anything voluntarily that was not in her house in two years. So of course, my expectation may have been in denial that she would show up for Thanksgiving. However, I wanted her to show up and thought she might. You can see where this is going.

She didn't come. I let it bother me. I was angry and let down. I tried to snap out of it, but it really was bothering me. I was pissed. Mostly I was pissed at myself because I had gotten my hopes up.

Sometime shortly after we ate Thanksgiving dinner, I went into the living room and attempted an inversion yoga move where I swing my legs up; it's called a chin-stand. I had been wanting to "get it" for a while. I was practicing. This time as I swung my legs fully up, the coffee table and my toes met on the way down. Ow! The yoga move produced a swollen, broken toe and a month of no shoes on that foot.

I knew this "accident" was not an accident. I was in a bad mood and trying to process my anger and sadness. I was mad. I had said words I didn't want to say to her in the process. My foot and the broken toe were a pause from the Universe to pay attention internally and not go down the frustration, sadness, and blame rabbit hole. It was a nice painful nudge to regroup.

When we don't consciously regroup, we will get an unconscious nudge or shove to do it anyway. Our bodies will continually give us these nudges. It's important to pay attention internally, and when that isn't clear, just look at our lives and our bodies. What are they telling you? Where can you regroup?

Reflection: Do you want to know how to interpret your life and body better and get the subtle nudges? A favorite book of mine is Louise Hay's *You Can Heal Your Life*. Learning to read your state and what you're feeling and create change is a powerful practice. There is massive power in the ability to reframe and regroup.

CHAPTER 38

TRAJECTORIES

I love traveling. Since I opened my practice in 2010, I have traveled all over the world. Service trips to Haiti have been a way to give back to the world, and I have gone a handful of times.

I enjoy going frequently because the mission goes to the same region several times a year; I am able to witness the change and improvement in the region we serve year to year!

During my second trip, I was prepared for what we were going to do and what I was going to see. This trip however, I got to witness the power of chiropractic, the power of adjustments, and how fast the body can experience a healing or shift.

A paralyzed older man who had had a stroke and was in a wheelchair was wheeled into our makeshift chiro clinic. He had a family member who came with him to our makeshift clinic.

Our translators told us that he had had the stroke two years before, he hadn't been able to move his legs or arms. His hands were curled into fists and arms clenched to his body.

An hour before, my team had arrived for the day and set up in this remote area. This man was one of the first patients of the day. One of the other practitioners was concerned about her ability to help him due to the severity of his body and lack of movement.

I gently asked to her if she thought he had access to any other help. She said, "I don't know. Maybe." I could feel her apprehension. So then I asked if we could at least start with evaluating him and see if we could help. She began checking out his spine and came and talked to me about his upper cervical spine that was severely stressed and subluxated. We agreed she should start to work on him.

She gently gave him an adjustment. After, we had him rest for a few minutes so we could recheck him in a bit. When we came to reevaluate, we saw his right fingers had uncurled and were no longer balled up. Both of us saw this and raised our eyebrows. Interesting. We let him rest further and then continued to work on his spine.

Several hours later, after several adjustments (and we have the pictures to prove it), we watched him stand up out of his wheelchair and lift his arms. It was amazing to witness.

That day showed me a few things. The power of the body to heal. And the power of courage and belief; belief that you can help. I returned home again changed by Haiti. But this story doesn't stop here.

A few months after returning from Haiti, I was at a business conference I attended frequently. Each time at this seminar, we would write out goals for thirty minutes, review them, and rewrite and improve upon them and see which had been accomplished. I drew out my old list of goals (written before I had even gone to Haiti) and reread my old card.

I didn't realize that I had as one of my top career goals to "see a chiropractic miracle." I knew when I wrote that I wanted to see someone radically change almost instantly. I know chiropractic is powerful by nature. As people are getting care, I have gotten to witness many, many lives changed for the better. However, I wanted to see something that would make me think, *Wow, that's radical.*

Looking down at the card, I laughed. I had put this intention on paper months ago. I had forgotten it, and *look* what showed up when I was in Haiti! Amazing. The power of our intention and expectations is so strong.

So you would think the story ends there, but it doesn't. I went home and back to practice. Months went by. I was set to speak in England for a chiropractic group. I decided to share the story of seeing a chiropractic miracle and the power of the potential to heal that each patient has.

I flew home from the seminar and was back in practice for another few weeks. At the time, I was working with other female chiros who were new in practice. One asked me to send her some before and after scans (part of the exam we do for new patients and at reevaluations) so she could start to see what differences we notice after a series of care. I forget to send them to her the first day.

The next day, I get an envelope in the mail from England. It was several thank-you notes from patients outside of London who were recovering from having strokes. They had written to me to thank me for sharing my story. Their chiropractor had heard my story while at the conference. It had sparked an idea that perhaps he was not seeing them as frequently as he could be, and he started to check their spines multiple times a day. The results spoke for themselves. They were recovering more of their function. I had several notes handwritten from patients telling me about their improvements.

He also sent me an email that day with before and after scans to show their progress from their original exam. I had to just shake my head. At this point, I already recognized the interconnection we all have and the amazing energy that binds us all. However, when things like this happen, where you get to see shreds of the trajectory that your life path sets in motion for others, it's quite amazing. It's truly a spiderweb.

I laughed at his emailed scans that also reminded me that I needed to share scans with that younger chiropractor who had asked. All I could think was that something much bigger had my back and I must be on the right path.

This true story is one I use to point out a few things. One, this is happening all the time, whether we want to admit it or not (or can see it). Two, our energy, actions, and beliefs are setting the stage for what we attract. It's like trajectories coming off you. Little rockets. A ripple or a wave. Momentum.

Reflection: What trajectories are coming off you right now? Can you see any of them in those closest to you? What synchronicities have shown up for you in the last two months? Are you paying attention or brushing them off?

CHAPTER 39

2020 OPPORTUNITIES

So here we are humans. I am getting these moments to write right now because I am working less due to the COVID-19 situation and taking some time to just be while I am in my last trimester of pregnancy.

Yes, 2020 showed us some pretty wacky things. Ultimately, I think these happenings are symptoms of a culture of humans who have gotten radically out of balance with themselves and their power.

We are *all here* together because our tapestry (all of us) has gotten out of balance. This is a correction, and 2020 may have offered us a radical opportunity. It may happen fast or slow. But we are here together, in our mess, ready to take responsibility and unfold something better for our future humans.

This "virus" has offered change! What can be good about this change? A few things to think about. This shutdown/slowdown is doing just that. Allowing many of us the much-needed opportunity to slow down and connect inward. *Who am I? How out of balance were some of my values, energy, and time?*

What we have built up in our life until this point is right in our face. We are home with all of it. Do you like it? What have you taken stock of in your own arena? Your relationships? Your finances? Your family? Your work? Your levels of fears?

How do you feel about other humans right now? Scared? Mortified? Empathetic? Loving? Hopeful? Frustrated? This is a way to take a reading of your internal states. It also may be a mirror for internal work on acceptance and love and also motivation to help change occur.

It doesn't matter right now where you came from or if you believe mainstream media or every YouTube video you watch. We are truly, collectively in this situation together. Some of us have more struggle right now than others, but we are all feeling it.

We all hold more power than we think we do; however, this power comes from us not succumbing to the fear. See it. Feel it, and realize fear is not the truth. Realize your neighbor with or without their mask is your brother or sister. Realize that humans you will never meet have had their lives impacted across the board. Realize that someone who is suffering right now (whether with the virus, due to anger, or due to heartbreak from missing a loved one, job loss, etc.) is experiencing part of what makes us all human. These are human experiences and human emotions. We are part of each other.

You're still making great money? Good, but someone isn't. You're not afraid for your life? Someone is. You have not lost someone during this and not been able to hold a proper funeral? Someone has. And they are your brothers and sisters, too. You are operating within the laws and guidelines? Great. Someone else is standing up for what's best for them. No matter what, we are still brothers and sisters. Politicians. You guessed it—part of our human family.

We are an organism together that is going through a massive healing. And it ain't comfortable. But healing rarely is. Something is getting purged right now. What have you been exposed to? What are you possibly thinking differently about now? Maybe this exposure had already been knocking on your door for years. Is that possible? There is much about our "old" way of living that was not harmonizing well. Not harmonizing for families, finances, political systems, healthcare, inflation—you name it.

Just like a fever ramps up in a body that needs to clean out and burn out the toxins, we are going through a cleansing process, I believe. Though the symptoms are uncomfortable, I am hopeful. We have lost touch with Mother Nature and her Intelligence. This Intelligence that animates our world is taking us for a ride right now—a collective fever, if you will.

So I am looking at this as an opportunity. I am willing to be uncomfortable (whether slightly or highly) if it means we end up in a much better place. I trust we will.

I am putting faith in stepping into more truth. More of our natural world to shine through. More of our natural ways of living to come back to us. Help us tune back in to *life*.

Much of our old "norm" had destruction written all over it. We had been tricked to think power comes from outside of us. From big jobs, big bills, big debt, and massive gluttony. We have lost touch with where true power is. We also have been tricked to think brothers and sisters on the other side of our world are not the same as us. We had been tricked to think a potion or pill is our savior for healing. We had been tricked to think that life is better lived through a screen with accolades of comments for every accomplishment or that a photoshopped life moment is what life is about. We have been tricked into thinking that if we avoid talking about death, it's not coming. It is. So we'd better learn to live *full* of life while we are here.

Just like a heart that is not beating in sync, the more we fractionate and pit ourselves against others, the more unharmonious or dis-eased we become. Yes, I think this scenario that is unfolding is offering a great benefit to us all. We have all been impacted by this, across the world. As we move out of violence, anger, despair, and fear, we can rationally make better, more informed choices for how we move our planet forward.

Each week that life moves forward in this new wavelength, I have been super-surprised at the conversations happening in my practice. More in-depth conversations and deeper-level discussions with people than I have ever had before. More people listening to many voices and weighing information with their own internal "true north."

We are most powerful as a population (American or world population) when we can agree to disagree and not have to be right at the expense of our brothers and sisters.

Reflection: Is there something that you are railing against right now? Is there any way for you to see the humanity in these instances instead of anger, fear, rage, etc.? Remember, whatever you pour your energy into (or focus on) expands! Do you like what you're energizing?

WHAT IF

What if everything is conspiring for my greatest good, for my greatest evolution, for my greatest purpose in this lifetime?

What if I am more in control of myself and my outcomes than I ever knew possible? What if I am more powerful and empowered than I ever believed?

CHAPTER 40

CHOICES

In my office, I have many ideas and recommendations to help someone heal and create different health and a different life. However, I don't get to choose for them. I don't get to rearrange their values so they line up with mine or what I think they should be. I also don't get to experience what they have lived that has brought them to this point.

They have choices. I have choices. No matter what, though, we can hold space for people. I believe that everyone who sets foot in the office is meant to be there. I don't know why or for how long, but they are there for a purpose.

I hold this belief for everything and everyone. That includes my staff, my patients, my family...really anyone. That doesn't mean I think all my patients will follow my recommendations. Quite the opposite. That is their choice, not mine. All I can do is my best job at teaching and serving and hold space for them to choose new paths. They will do what's best for themselves. That's not up to me.

Same thought process with my staff. I have had people who are with me for a long time and we have been through some thick and thin together. We have had many learning curves together. I don't get to control what happens as we move forward. Maybe we will continue to grow together. Maybe we will grow apart. Values can change. Our office will continue to change. That's okay.

As a leader in my practice and community, I may have to make hard choices, use my voice at times to speak up for what is needed, and move our mission forward to help more people and do it congruently to our vision. You can be a compassionate leader and still have a strong voice, strong action, and strong boundaries.

Each of us has choices to make. I am responsible for my own choices. You are responsible for yours. This type of thinking has set me free. I try to apply it in all aspects of my life. Some areas are easier than others.

When I was not applying this, it was easy to drown. Life the first year my mom was sick and not taking care of herself was very hard. I wanted to fix her. I wanted to do the work for her. Ultimately, her responsibilities are not mine. When we get out of balance with this, we struggle and become unhealthy. When we let others be fully responsible for their choices and actions, that is empowering. You are allowing them their choices. You are also freeing yourself.

> Reflection: Where are you trying to control or take responsibility for others? We must be careful to hold space and also know when to voice our truth, our opinion, and to recognize when our own action needs to happen regardless of others. By doing this, we set others free to do the same.

CHAPTER 41

PART OF THE WHOLE

To start to make small shifts, we can make choices that are good for us and good for our world. These send out big ripples. Maybe you are going to take care of your body more. Maybe you are going to cook healthier meals for your family. Maybe you are going to choose to cut back on waste leaving your house.

The first week of the quarantine, my son, husband, youngest stepdaughter, and I walked down our neighborhood street and picked up five bags of trash in about a one-mile stretch. I commented to my husband that 90 percent of it was alcohol-related garbage. Discarded out of cars or people walking. Saddening.

Then, as the lake that we live on opened up, we walked down to the rocks and were looking out at the lake. The ice had just left.

My husband saw an orange and clear tube. It looked like garbage. A discarded needle for injections. He carefully cleaned it up. I was again saddened as I thought, *What if that was down in the sand where my son swims?* I thought about our connection to our earth, what we carelessly have done at times as humans to Mother Earth, and our own connection to her and our own temples (our bodies).

This is not me on my high horse. This is me saying Mother Nature will move forward and correct our species with or without the human population. We must make some new choices and get back in tune.

We are not smarter than nature. We are not separate from nature; some of us have lost touch. And if a portion of us have, we all have. It is like once your cells start to go rogue (we call that cancer). There is disharmony in the normal ecosystem of the body. It may be an intelligent response but at the expense of the life of the organism. Humanity, we need to pay attention. Our death is not the end of Mother Earth.

Help each other. Tune back in. First to ourselves. The microcosm in each of us matters. Begin to choose our thoughts wisely. Think deeply about how we choose to treat our bodies and view our bodies as part of our "whole."

Reflection: As we respect and honor our inner world and our outer world, we can start to see the connection. As I clear my own judgments and fear internally, I am doing a service for humanity. As I clear my external world of clutter, it also shifts my inner world. The microcosm and macrocosm reflect each other. Energy is intertwined. It is so beautiful.

CHAPTER 42

SHIT STORMS

Massive lessons and change can come disguised as shit storms. In 2020, I saw who on my team was committed to being there and where I needed to train about our philosophy deeper, where my finances could stretch, where I could cut back in money, business, and personal accounts.

I also saw new opportunities to help others. Time opened up to play more and snuggle more with Jack. Time opened up for writing this book. Time was (and is) available for organizing and nesting for a baby. I felt a desire to be home more than I ever had before. These are all things I wanted to do, but a massive pattern interruption like COVID-19 accelerated all of it. Find the good; see the good. Keep the good in focus.

I again do not mean to Pollyanna this time period. I know it's been an extremely challenging time for many on different levels. For me, I have had some nightmares after watching some of the freedoms be stripped away and paying attention to politics more than ever.

I have distanced myself from the phone and some of the documentaries I was viewing because I could feel my system in fight or flight. Not a great "state" for growing a baby. However, I keep coming back to this hope that it is unfolding as it should.

There are so many blessings to be offered. I just have to look for them. Not stare at the fact that there may be fewer people coming into our business, or that we are not hitting our business goals I had laid out at the beginning of the year.

There is the overwhelm we feel in life's shit storms. We are in our head thinking so much that sometimes we forget we are not in control of everything and everyone.

Currently, I am trying to figure out how to keep all my staff working depending on what happens and respond to incessant emails from others who are also looking for similar help and guidance for their businesses. Can we stay open? What do we need to do differently due to these circumstances? Did new mandates change? What are others doing? How is my community going to react?

You see, *that* is the overwhelm. When we stare at those unknown things, it's easy to be drained. I do it too. We all can go there. I go there. When you feel that point of frustration and overwhelm, that is a great time to take a pause. Regroup and pivot. I am going to serve *everyone* (including myself) better if I take a break or pause (even for ten minutes) and regroup.

COVID-19 is not the first time any of us have experienced these "holy shit" moments. It just may be the first time we have experienced something that feels so out of our control and is impacting everyone on almost every front. We may not be the same as our neighbor, but we are all likely experiencing challenges.

I trust now more than I ever had. That there is an Intelligence unfolding at *all times*. Even if that Intelligence is creating chaos. It has created me. It is growing that small baby in my belly. It is more powerful than any system, government, virus, or fear, and my reverence for that makes me want to take its nudges. Lean in. Lead with my connection to this Intelligence. Get quiet and listen to it.

For whatever reason, for whatever conspiracy/truth I choose to believe about COVID-19, the effects this season of life has had on the world are monumental. Scary virus or not, this spell of time is leaving a deep imprint on us all. We get to choose how it nudges us. What patterns is it showing you? What patterns are you breaking? What is waking up?

If we feel too unsafe, chances are we are deep in fight or flight, curled up in a ball, or syphoning off more fear from all of our devices and the people around us. If we can shut that off and get safe in our system, we will be able to pivot much easier.

Breathe. Do some yoga. Get on the grass. Move your body. Get some sunshine. We can remember this truth: we are all in this together. That the *Universe* is more powerful than this virus and we are made up of this Intelligence.

That is my message for this whole book. I am using the moments of my life (the highlights and the bloopers so hopefully you can relate to your own life experiences) to show this point: trust this Intelligence that is unfolding in your life, and put your energy into what *you* want. Surround yourself more often with life-giving people, resources, and attitudes, and life can become magical, even in this current state.

Then, when you can see those magical moments, when you can

feel that your internal system is safe and grounded, make new decisions. Trust those times.

When you are freaking out, it is *not* the time to make decisions about anything. Don't send that email. Don't say those words. Pause instead. Those states are destructive states.

You don't have to believe me. Look at someone who seems angry (or fearful, resentful, shameful, guilty, or uncertain) most of the time; what is the rest of their life like? Would you trade?

Their point of attraction in a dominant place of anger can only create more aggression (or whatever their dominant state is) in their life. Want to change your life? Surround yourself with more people who live in dominant states you would like yourself. Want to keep your life stuck? Stick around with people you would not like to trade lives with.

It is law. Universal law: you and your life are a reflection of what you are on the inside. Accepting this is true is a major step in change.

So what could you respond to differently in your life?

Reflection: In the midst of a shit storm, how do you reconnect? How do you respond? What is your point of attraction? Are you the storm?

CHAPTER 43

STICK YOUR NECK OUT

A couple of nights before I wrote this chapter (in 2020), my husband and I were discussing current events and, you know, the world.

I consider myself a free thinker, so I said to him, "We have to stand up for our rights to our bodies." Which also made me chuckle, because my four-year-old has been learning the phrase and what it means. His line from daycare is: "I am in charge of my body."

Now he says that to me when I ask him to try certain things for dinner and he doesn't want to or I tell him it's bedtime. A chip off the old block. My dad says it's karma. I don't want to break this in him. Both of us may be a bit high strung.

Anyway, as we were discussing our medical rights and some of the worldwide agendas that may be happening; Kyle sighed and said, "We don't have any control anyway."

Instantly, a nerve was struck by that comment. I cannot and will not believe this. No matter what. Everything I have learned these past years has made me believe we have every right to an empowered life. I also believe that one person can create a ripple that changes the world, so I refuse to think this way.

Does this mean making positive changes will be easy? No. Does this mean it will come without opposition? No. Probably more than we all can see. Does it mean you won't have to stick your neck out? No again.

Sticking your neck out can make people very uncomfortable. Rattling old beliefs and old structures can also feel really weird. But think back to people who have been willing, as one person or a small group of people, to start something bigger than what the masses said was possible. Martin Luther King Jr. Gandhi. Mother Theresa. The Wright brothers. Einstein. You have to be able to see things differently for humanity in order to change humanity. It's generally not warm, fuzzy, and comfortable. Loving actions can be met with resistance. That doesn't mean stop.

From my point of view, I would love to see the opportunity that 2020 has brought us spark a transition into much change that has been brewing. I would ask these changes of myself and others.

I would love to see our politicians work for the people again. To see new protections put in place so that those making our rules and running our world will not have their pockets heavily lined with billions from their political agendas. A return to politicians who care for their constituents and ultimately this country and true freedom. Is that too much to ask? I don't think so.

I would like to see transparency at a new level. From one-on-

one to our biggest corporations. I would like to see *big* pharma held accountable for the deceit and manipulation of people's lives and loved ones. We are promoted a message of doom about our body, and that needs to end.

I would like the truth widely publicized that science is not settled. Ever. We are constantly relearning and rewriting "science." People then could stop throwing science up like it's settled law and cannot be challenged.

I would love to see people tapped into their natural world. Learning to trust their own inborn wisdom more than a pill or potion. Learning to see their bodies as magnificent and not broken.

I would love to see each person remember this deep wisdom they carry. Learning to trust in their own intuition and sense of purpose and letting it lead their lives. Not just posting their lives up on social media but really *living* them.

I would love to see more people thrive by following their life calling and not staying in jobs they hate to pay bills and taxes or to keep good insurance. Good insurance wouldn't matter if we fixed our broken, corrupt healthcare system and its terrible messages about our bodies.

I'd love to see so much of the *how* to be successful break down. Break the pattern of "You must follow these structures or else. Be good. Raise your hand. Go to school. Go to college. Get a job. Work it long and hard, and retire. Save your money so when you retire you can live." That needs to change.

We could learn to glorify a life that is lived more in the present moments. Less materialism and more *life* with people and ideas and purpose we love.

I would love to see people consciously using media. Remembering to tune it out at periods. Limiting the "programming" they are receiving from any source. Remember a post is not a spelled-out conversation. That attacking someone else rarely leads to change.

I would love to see people realize Mother Nature is really our mother. To take care of her differently, make a one- or two-degree shift in how they handle their consumerism and waste.

I would love to see women and men honor their bodies and each other and recognize we all have masculine and feminine energies. Honor aging and life experience. Honor the wisdom that is present in all of life.

I'd love to see a renaissance back to safer, less invasive birth practices and cultivate empowered feminine and masculine energies in all of us. I'd love to see women and men supported to embrace the rawness of new life, birth, and pregnancy, not as a medical emergency, but as a miracle unfolding in a natural process.

I would like to see some of the new technology for safer energy and safer farming actually be embraced instead of silencing these ideas just so the old ways and money structures stay in power. Again, this goes back to more transparency and ability to follow the money.

Maybe this is all pie in the sky; however, now that I know our minds access the collective mind together, holding a dream or prayer to me is conjuring up a better future that can be accessed and created by us all together. It is far more productive to hold life-producing thoughts than stare at the negative and think we are all doomed. *I know these changes start with me.*

I do believe that this pause we are having is a great opportunity to *wake up*. I believe it's your soul calling you back to truth. The truth that change is inevitable.

Your higher self is in alignment with love, connection, truth, joy, and freedom. When we are connected to these principles, there is more energy available to us. These higher states are massively influential. As the collective of humanity awakens, change is happening.

So I leave you with this. Connect to yourself first. Do what fills your cup. Do what helps you to stay healthy and whole. Then, dream and plan. Take action. Stick your neck out. Rest. And repeat.

> Reflection: So I challenge you: how would you like the world to be like in ten years? How can your life be part of creating this? It starts with each of us.

CHAPTER 44

DO SOMETHING, KID. EVEN IF IT'S WRONG!

I have shared a lot with you about my life in the past ten years, and I want to underline a few things to make them crystal clear.

I don't know your life. However, I do believe these principles can apply to anyone. By the nature of us all being united in humanity, we share this bond of being electromagnetic, and our energy and our state matters to what we are creating. We are walking magnets.

Someone who complains and is grumpy all the time—their life and worldview mirrors that. Someone who can make lemonade out of lemons seems to have a lucky horseshoe. Someone who dreams and knows their life can be magical has a magical life. Really, they just are sending out different energy, and the Universe is matching it.

Line up your thoughts. Take a new path. Make a degree shift in some of your beliefs. The definition of insanity is doing the same thing and expecting a different result.

Don't know what to do? My grandfather used to always tell us, "Do something, kid. Even if it's wrong." What I think he meant was: don't sit on your ass; go for something. Think, dream, and then take an action. Do not be immobilized by having to have it all figured out.

I have found that by operating this way, you make some moves that don't work out; however, you find out faster which ones will work and which ones won't. Navigating becomes easier again because you have momentum with you. You are not just sitting waiting for the perfect time.

Create something? Great! What's the next step? Don't know how to do it? Find someone who does, but keep it moving forward. No one is going to do it for you, nor should they. You will have a lot of help along the way that you attract as your momentum grows.

Also, do not let money be the thing that stops you. Learn that if money is your excuse for not doing things, it may be time to put some energy into listening to podcasts, books, and seminars that teach about abundance and becoming better at money habits. An education nowadays can be basically free with all the podcasts and YouTube channels out there. Get educated.

This concept of looking at money as an exchange of energy can be really helpful. If you can help others, you can make money. If you can do more "work" and be of "service" with more energy and more of *you* (and your gifts) compared to where you are currently, the Universe will reward you. It is the law of exchange.

Don't believe me? Look at your life. The amount of effort and energy you are actually expanding into the universe and others (instead of me, me, me) will show up in your life. If you can improve your ability to receive abundance, this will be radically helpful. Some of us have a hard time with this concept, so abundance comes to us in other ways.

Lastly, we all have negative thoughts. We all have trials and tribulations. We all have periods of our life that are not going to be glamorous and may be gut-wrenching. These periods offer strength; you are forged by the fire. Can you shed what doesn't serve you, learn, and become like a tree that keeps growing and bends with the wind, or do you snap?

To allow your frustration and not be won over by it. To allow your pain, and not let it break you. To fail at one thing and realize it's not the end of the story. Learn to allow, take stock of where you are, and move on. And keep on dreaming of the next step you are going to *do*!

We are not going to ever get "done." We are a sliver in this tapestry, but that does not make us insignificant. Our energy in the field is important. For our own life, those connected to us and those we will never meet. Do not be discouraged by trials, tribulations, and things that come out of left field. There is still order. This snapshot we have in our moment right now is just one small sliver of what is unfolding. Sometimes it is helpful to remember this as you work on your level of acceptance and stepping into the new.

I will keep moving. I will tune within and then take the next step to create. I will be doing all these steps right along with you.

Thank you for reading about the evolution of my life. I would

love to hear more about your own reclamation. I can only imagine where the next ten years or so will lead to. Hugs!

P.S. Friends, you can find more from me at drlonacook.com.

ACKNOWLEDGMENTS

I would love to honor my mother. As my new baby, Max, is now birthed into this world, my mom has taken a new interest in him. I can visit her, and she sits up and holds him. This has been so healing for me to see. I would like to acknowledge her willingness to listen to me read the edits of this book out loud so I can process what still needs to be worked on. Thank you, Mom. I love you and all you have done for me over my lifetime. I am grateful for the life and experiences we have shared.

I also would like to acknowledge my hubs, Kyle, who continually puts up with me and my creations. He also lets me read out loud and is a dream supporter. Thanks, Klocko! Love you.

I would like to shout out to Nana Wald and Amanda Haines. Thanks for reading, editing, and giving feedback in the early stages of the book. Thanks for all you bring into my life!

Lastly, my boys (especially Max) who lay on the bed with me in early hours editing. XO, XO! I love you both to the moon and outer planets and beyond. I can't just say moon because Jack says it's not that far away. I also can't say, "Love you to pieces," because Jack says that sounds mean.

ABOUT THE AUTHOR

LONA COOK is an author, a chiropractor, and a firm believer in personal growth and holistic health. A thriving entrepreneur, she has been practicing since 2010 in Chippewa Falls, Wisconsin, where she lives with her husband and two sons.

Her greatest passion lies in helping others recognize the Intelligence in their mind, body, and spirit, so they can apply that innate guidance throughout their lives and reach their own highest potential.

Find her at www.drlonacook.com.